"In an age when ...., ...ng' in a mysterious, individualistic, and job-oriented way, Klein and Steiner bring us back to the essence of biblical calling—believers are called in Christ to be the people of God and to live accordingly before the Lord and in community with one another. Returning to this central sense of calling can be refreshing, life enhancing, and transformative for Christians who struggle with confusion or even the fear that they have missed God's calling for their lives. I heartily recommend this book."

—**Donald Fairbairn**, Gordon-Conwell Theological Seminary

"Like many other Christian notions, 'calling' is plagued by ambiguity. Its popular understanding is imprecise, and the term is often conveniently used to affirm our self-appointed vocations. Without God, a call is merely a task done ostensibly in Christ's name. We cannot handle calling so glibly; it is too essential. Using top-shelf biblical and theological insight, Klein and Steiner provide a gracious and uncompromising course correction. They underline the mission that is common to all believers: God the caller has invited us into fellowship with Christ and commissioned us to glorify him. I commend *What Is My Calling?* to all who desire biblical and theological clarity on their divine purpose."

—**Brandon Washington**, pastor, The Embassy Church

"The desire to understand one's calling is particularly important for students in Bible colleges and seminaries, so this book is a must-read for their professors and mentors. However, this study shows that calling is also a crucial issue for every believer. Drawing the meaning of calling directly from the New Testament, Klein and Steiner show that our calling is in Christ, and they place it in the context of corporate identity and character rather than in a specific ministry, job, task, or role. They provide relevant and pragmatic applications for living out our call as well as healthy correctives to past and present misunderstandings of calling."

—**Cynthia Long Westfall**, McMaster Divinity College

"Does God promise to call you if he wants you in ministry? Does one receive a calling to a secular job? What if I have a great opportunity that sounds like something I would enjoy and am good at and that would help the Lord's work, but I have never had the slightest feeling of a calling? Are any of these questions even legitimate when judged by the Bible's usage of the concept of calling? Klein and Steiner draw on years of study and ministry to set the record straight. Their answers should encourage many, many Christians, while challenging some who have spoken wrongly on these matters. This is must-reading for anyone who cares about God's will for their life."

—**Craig L. Blomberg**, Denver Seminary

WHAT IS MY CALLING?

A BIBLICAL and THEOLOGICAL EXPLORATION of CHRISTIAN IDENTITY

WILLIAM W. KLEIN AND DANIEL J. STEINER

Baker Academic

a division of Baker Publishing Group
Grand Rapids, Michigan

© 2022 by William W. Klein and Daniel J. Steiner

Published by Baker Academic
a division of Baker Publishing Group
PO Box 6287, Grand Rapids, MI 49516-6287
www.bakeracademic.com

Printed in the United States of America

Library of Congress Cataloging-in-Publication Data
Names: Klein, William W. (William Wade) author. | Steiner, Daniel J., 1980– author.
Title: What is my calling? : a biblical and theological exploration of Christian identity / William W. Klein and Daniel J. Steiner.
Description: Grand Rapids, Michigan : Baker Academic, a division of Baker Publishing Group, [2022] | Includes bibliographical references and index.
Identifiers: LCCN 2021040503 | ISBN 9781540963079 (paperback) | ISBN 9781540965301 (casebound) | ISBN 9781493434862 (ebook) | ISBN 9781493434879 (pdf)
Subjects: LCSH: Vocation—Christianity. | Identity (Psychology)—Religious aspects—Christianity.
Classification: LCC BV4740 .K548 2022 | DDC 248.4—dc23
LC record available at https://lccn.loc.gov/2021040503

Baker Publishing Group publications use paper produced from sustainable forestry practices and post-consumer waste whenever possible.

22 23 24 25 26 27 28   7 6 5 4 3 2 1

As husbands and fathers,
we strive to demonstrate our
calling in Christ to our wives and children.
In gratitude for them, we dedicate this book to

Phyllis, Alison, and Sarah

Anna, Josiah, Micah, and Cambria

I press on toward the goal to win the prize for which God has called me heavenward in Christ Jesus. (Phil. 3:14)

As a prisoner for the Lord, then, I urge you to live a life worthy of the calling you have received. (Eph. 4:1)

Contents

Preface

We are theological educators. We take the word "education" seriously. We do not engage in indoctrination, telling our students what to believe and how to think. Our mission entails helping our students develop critical skills that will equip them to think biblically and theologically, and as a result to live and minister as authentic and faithful followers of Jesus Christ. As authors, we two inhabit what are often seen as rival departments: biblical/theological (Bill, a professor of New Testament) versus praxis (Dan, a professor of Training and Mentoring and leadership coach). Often in popular thinking, theology and biblical studies inhabit an ivory tower and are largely irrelevant to how common folk live. Others wonder if the "practical departments" lack academic rigor and are driven by cultural trends or fads. In our view, no such divide exists (in fact, Dan has a ThM in theology), for we are convinced that biblical truth (or theology) is eminently practical, and we strive to help our students integrate both worlds.

A couple decades ago, Laura Flanders, then teaching in the Training and Mentoring (T/M) department of Denver Seminary, recruited Bill to develop and offer a seminar to graduating students in the final semester of their study. The assigned topic was "Calling." The T/M department realized how confused many students felt about the topic, especially while they were seeking ministry positions upon graduation. How would they know they were called to a specific church or other ministry opportunity? What if no job opened up for them? Did they miss their calling or wrongly suppose that God had called them? As a result, Bill designed and refined a seminar over the years; it eventually was videoed and continues to be used by the T/M courses in various ways.

Then, several years ago while Dan was teaching and mentoring in that department, he approached Bill and asked if we might collaborate to write a book together that (1) expanded Bill's seminar and grounded it more solidly in the Scriptures, (2) developed a more robust theological understanding for calling, and (3) provided practical help for our students and the larger community of believers in their various walks of life. After several wide-ranging conversations, we agreed to this project, believing that such a book could help Christians understand this important topic. Why? We are convinced that the word "calling" is greatly misused and misunderstood in today's world. And we believe that a biblically robust understanding will encourage and benefit all Christians—including *you*, the reader—"to live a life worthy of the calling you have received." A limited or anemic understanding of calling robs the church of the contributions of all God's people to God's mission in the world. This volume represents our offering to the church, with prayers that God's Spirit will use it to enable us all to understand and live out our calling in Christ.

We offer our thanks to Laura Flanders for her initial collaboration with Bill in thinking more deeply about our calling in Christ. We are also grateful for Laura's influence on Dan as a professor, mentor, leader, and colleague; he would not be who he is today without her affirmation and encouragement. She also read parts of this manuscript, and her input improved our thinking, especially on the topic of mentoring.

We are grateful for those who have helped shape many of the ideas in this book. To our seminary students throughout the years:

your personal stories, inquisitive minds, and gracious pushbacks have expanded our understanding and appreciation of God's call on our lives. To those involved in "5280 Fellowship" cohorts: thanks for your vulnerability and willingness to explore the topic of calling as it relates to the whole of your lives.[1] You are making a difference in Denver and beyond for the sake of Christ and others!

And to our colleagues, mentors, and friends who encourage us and exemplify what it means to live out our calling to Christ—Brian Gray, Ryan Tafilowski, Dale Flanders, Don Payne, David Buschart, Erin Heim, Luke Sawyer, Rob Chestnut, Emmanuel Engulu, Debra Anderson, Jeff and Lianne Nikkel, and Jeff Haanen—thank you for your influence and support in our lives.

We are grateful that Baker Academic recognized this as a worthy project, and we especially thank Bryan Dyer and Wells Turner for their oversight of this work.

Bill Klein
Dan Steiner

1. The 5280 Fellowship (https://5280fellows.com/) is a nine-month program in spiritual formation, professional development, and civic influence that forms Christian professionals to serve God, neighbor, and society through their work.

Abbreviations

General and Bibliographic

/	or
//	parallel to
ANF	*The Ante-Nicene Fathers*. Edited by Alexander Roberts and James Donaldson. 10 vols. New York: Christian Literature, 1885–96. Reprint, Grand Rapids: Eerdmans, 1950–51.
BDAG	*A Greek-English Lexicon of the New Testament and Other Early Christian Literature*. By Walter Bauer, Frederick W. Danker, William F. Arndt, and F. Wilbur Gingrich. 3rd ed. Chicago: University of Chicago Press, 2000.
CEB	Common English Bible
chap(s).	chapter(s)
CSB	Christian Standard Bible
EDNT	*Exegetical Dictionary of the New Testament*. Edited by Horst Balz and Gerhard Schneider. 3 vols. Grand Rapids: Eerdmans, 1990–93.
ed(s).	edition, editor(s)
e.g.	*exempli gratia*, for example
esp.	especially
ESV	English Standard Version
et al.	*et alii*, and others
exp.	expanded
Gk.	Greek
HALOT	*The Hebrew and Aramaic Lexicon of the Old Testament*. By Ludwig Koehler, Walter Baumgartner, and Johann J. Stamm. 3rd ed. 5 vols. Leiden: Brill, 1994–2001.

Hb.	Hebrew
i.e.	*id est*, that is
KJV	King James Version
LXX	Septuagint
NABRE	New American Bible (Revised Edition)
NASB	New American Standard Bible
NET	New English Translation
NIDNTTE	*New International Dictionary of New Testament Theology and Exegesis*. Edited by Moisés Silva. 5 vols. Grand Rapids: Zondervan, 2014.
NIDOTTE	*New International Dictionary of Old Testament Theology and Exegesis*. Edited by Willem A. VanGemeren. 5 vols. Grand Rapids: Zondervan, 1997.
NIV	New International Version (2011)
NJB	New Jerusalem Bible
NRSV	New Revised Standard Version
NT	New Testament
OT	Old Testament
p(p).	page(s)
par(r).	parallel(s) (as in the Gospels) = //
rev.	revised
TDOT	*Theological Dictionary of the Old Testament*. Edited by G. Johannes Botterweck and Helmer Ringgren. Translated by John T. Willis et al. 15 vols. Grand Rapids: Eerdmans, 1974–2018.
trans.	translation, translated by
vol(s).	volumes
WA	Weimarer Ausgabe = [Martin Luther's Works, in Latin and German, complete critical ed.]. Weimar: Hermann Böhlau and H. Böhlaus Nachfolger, 1883–2009.

Old Testament

Gen.	Genesis	2 Kings	2 Kings
Exod.	Exodus	1 Chron.	1 Chronicles
Lev.	Leviticus	2 Chron.	2 Chronicles
Num.	Numbers	Ezra	Ezra
Deut.	Deuteronomy	Neh.	Nehemiah
Josh.	Joshua	Esther	Esther
Judg.	Judges	Job	Job
Ruth	Ruth	Ps(s).	Psalm(s)
1 Sam.	1 Samuel	Prov.	Proverbs
2 Sam.	2 Samuel	Eccles.	Ecclesiastes
1 Kings	1 Kings	Song	Song of Songs

Isa.	Isaiah	Jon.	Jonah
Jer.	Jeremiah	Mic.	Micah
Lam.	Lamentations	Nah.	Nahum
Ezek.	Ezekiel	Hab.	Habakkuk
Dan.	Daniel	Zeph.	Zephaniah
Hosea	Hosea	Hag.	Haggai
Joel	Joel	Zech.	Zechariah
Amos	Amos	Mal.	Malachi
Obad.	Obadiah		

New Testament

Matt.	Matthew	1 Tim.	1 Timothy
Mark	Mark	2 Tim.	2 Timothy
Luke	Luke	Titus	Titus
John	John	Philem.	Philemon
Acts	Acts	Heb.	Hebrews
Rom.	Romans	James	James
1 Cor.	1 Corinthians	1 Pet.	1 Peter
2 Cor.	2 Corinthians	2 Pet.	2 Peter
Gal.	Galatians	1 John	1 John
Eph.	Ephesians	2 John	2 John
Phil.	Philippians	3 John	3 John
Col.	Colossians	Jude	Jude
1 Thess.	1 Thessalonians	Rev.	Revelation
2 Thess.	2 Thessalonians		

Other Ancient Writings

1–2 Clem.	1–2 Clement
Herm. Sim.	Shepherd of Hermas, Similitudes

Introduction

In the Christian world today (and in the larger culture as well), the words "call" and "calling" frequently occur. We hear that people feel called to all kinds of things. People are encouraged to find their calling or vocation in life, to find and follow their passion. For some, a job fills the bill; they believe they are working in their calling. Others find their vocation elsewhere, though it often needs to be pursued or discovered. The same ideas overlap the religious realm. Church search committees or ministerial assessment bodies often—apparently invariably—seek to discover if a candidate is "called" to the ministry at large, to a specific church, or to a position. Seminaries market their programs by promising to help prepare graduates to fulfill God's calling on their lives. Some people say that God called them to pastoral ministry, the mission field, or to work with orphans, and the list could go on and on. Yet for many people, any idea of calling lies completely outside their experience. It is an irrelevant concept.

Doesn't it all seem so subjective and confusing? In our work with seminary students and local Fellows programs particularly, we find that some can articulate a clear sense of calling, others cannot, and still others struggle to know what that means. Should the absence of a conviction of God's calling disqualify people from pursuing Christian ministries? When candidates for ministry are up for appointment, do we take their word for it that they have experienced a call? How do we know that our definition of calling lines up with theirs? What about those who are not pursuing occupational ministry positions? How does "calling" apply to their pursuits, if at all? If it does apply, is this calling different from those in professional ministry settings? Is there some mechanism or inventory to determine accurately whether someone genuinely possesses a call—assuming that everyone understands "calling" in the same way?

Both of us have worked extensively in and with local churches (including as pastors and elders) over many years, and we have observed both the presence and absence of a clear sense of calling among people in ministry and people in the pews. The presence or absence of a sense of calling does not seem to determine whether someone is successful or effective in ministry—again, whether lay or professional.

In response to these questions, we decided to pursue this topic in more depth. How shall we understand and use the word "calling"? This book embodies what we have learned together. In short, we conclude that all Christians have a calling in Christ that defines their identity and mission as they engage the varied contexts and circumstances of their lives. Calling should be applied to and lived out within our varied jobs, tasks, and roles, but it should not be equated to these particular and often-changing dimensions of our lives. We think that the church and church leaders (our intended targets) too often have misconstrued how the Bible understands the important topic of calling and that many popular and well-meaning presentations of calling miss the mark when set alongside the biblical evidence. Popular understandings often lack any theological support or basis; they are often anecdotal and based solely on personal experiences. These highly subjective uses of calling terminology may work for some people, leading them to a sense of faithfulness, flourishing, and well-being in the world.

But when inspected objectively and held alongside the biblical text, such popular uses of calling are found to be unbiblical and often lead to frustration, hurt, angst, division, and confusion. Instead, our calling to Christ is intended to lead to freedom and unity. Although we cannot control how others use words, we believe there is much to be gained when Christians understand what the Bible says about their calling and express it accurately.

The book proceeds as follows. In chapter 1 we survey the landscape of calling by exploring how contemporary writers and speakers use the ideas of calling and vocation. We examine various resources for which calling is the primary topic, as well as those that discuss calling as a subsidiary issue. While calling is often popularly portrayed as something positive, we consider the troublesome "shadow side" to uses of the term "calling." From these studies we will develop a taxonomy of the popular uses of calling among Christians today.

In chapter 2 we reflect on how the church has arrived at this point. We conduct a historical survey of how theologians have used the idea of calling over the past two thousand years. This survey provides context and insight as we seek to untangle ourselves from unhelpful, and even unbiblical, uses of calling language. William Placher's *Callings: Twenty Centuries of Christian Wisdom on Vocation* sets out a four-part historical framework that we will adopt for moving through the centuries up to the present.

In chapter 3 we consider the biblical evidence for calling. We explore how the concept of calling is used in both the OT and NT. This requires us to engage texts and passages that address germane concepts even where the words "call" or "calling" do not occur. For example, some passages that discuss God's "will," "appointment," or the verb "choose/elect" will prove relevant to unpacking an understanding of God's call on a person's life. A breakdown of individual studies will include (1) calling in the OT; (2) calling in the Gospels and Acts; (3) calling in the Epistles; and (4) God's will for people.

This background enables us, in chapter 4, to cross-examine the uses of calling language. First, we sort out the results of our biblical study. Then we compare these results with the ways in which writers through history portray "calling," using the taxonomy we developed in chapter 1. Since we aim to discover what meanings we should consider normative for Christians today, we determine how the two lists (biblical vs. current usage) match up. In an appendix we develop a list of the normative uses of calling in the Bible.

Chapter 5 is our attempt to construct a theological map for calling. First, we engage with some key theological thinkers to help us deconstruct many contemporary models. Miroslav Volf aids our critique of Martin Luther, who is often considered a key contributor to a theology of calling. In the end, we seek to construct a theological reorientation of calling that complements and reinforces the conclusions from our biblical studies. We believe that a theology of calling must work in real life for all Christians and not be merely theoretical or apply only to some people or some circumstances.

In chapter 6 we draw together our findings to show how a biblically based and theologically robust theology of calling can work in life and ministry today. Here we consider why calling language is so regularly and commonly misused today. Then we suggest a way forward, appealing to our fellow readers to embrace our true calling as Christians—and what that means in practical terms. We recommend ways to navigate the world of Christian ministry and wider avenues of service that embody our true calling in Christ.

1

The Landscape of Calling

Words shape culture, and culture shapes our words. Ten years ago, the word "selfie" was not a mainstay in our vocabulary. Perhaps someone somewhere uttered it by accident, but today it has reached such heights as being added to the list of acceptable words by Scrabble in 2014 and such lows as being the cause of over 250 deaths between 2011 and 2017.[1] A tangible example of "selfie-impact" on our culture can be seen in how taking a picture of oneself by oneself has revolutionized technology. One of us two authors got his first cell phone in 2001 while a college student. Then a cell phone was simply a device for making phone calls—no apps, games, music, or camera. Now our cell phones are "smart phones," containing all these features and much more. In fact, they contain two cameras: one on the front and one on the back. The camera on the opposite side of the screen is understandable, but why would a phone need a front-facing camera? Selfies, of course! From coffee-table books to the power of cultural influence through social media, we probably do not yet know to what extent selfies have shaped us as people and how we relate to others and the world around us. This is not a rant about the narcissistic tendencies

1. *BBC News*, "Selfie Deaths."

of our current historical moment. "Selfie" simply illustrates our point: words shape culture, and culture shapes our words.

As "selfie" is to our broader culture at large, "calling" is to our Christian subculture (and beyond). The notion of calling has shaped much of how Christians think about what it means to be a Christian and how to live the Christian faith in the world. That is, how this word has been adopted and used within the Christian world has shaped our understanding of its meaning and informed our very understanding of how to live faithfully as God's people. Consider, for example, the titles of a few articles from The Babylon Bee, a satirical news site that pokes fun at popular tendencies within Christian culture: "Man Mistakes Indigestion for Pastoral Call"; "Man Called to Mission Trip in Remote 'World of Warcraft' Jungle"; "Local Christian Just Not Feeling Called to Christian Virtue of Charity"; "Worship Leader Called by God to Be Famous, Wealthy." Satire is an effective form of criticism because it is based in truth and exposes the weaknesses and faults of its subject. What is The Babylon Bee revealing about our collective, functional understanding of calling? In the popular sense, "calling" is individual and subjective; it primarily relates to a job, task, or role (often a ministry one); and it can be used to justify personally motivated decisions. While this does not capture the full scope of "calling" in popular usage, it is functionally what the term means to many people. And most Christians have no reason to question this.

In this chapter we will illustrate, unmask, and question this very functional theology of calling. First, we will consider the shadow side of this popular use of calling terminology. Personal accounts are one of the strongest supports for how and why calling terminology is used. Many of these accounts paint calling in an affirmative and desirable light. This is not always the case, though, and these sorts of calling stories may actually be in the minority in the collective experience of God's people. Second, we will present a survey of how calling terminology is used in resources produced in the past twenty years. Based on this survey, we will devise a taxonomy of the popular uses of calling language, which in later chapters will be placed in conversation with biblical and theological studies of calling. Third, we will summarize the biblical support of the popular calling conversation, identifying primary hermeneutical strategies apparently employed within these recent resources. Finally, we will present some observations from the current landscape of calling, which will frame what is to come in the following chapters in this book.

The Shadow Side of Calling

Personal accounts are valuable for showing how the Christian community understands calling. These narratives tell how individuals have discovered a deeper sense of purpose and meaning in life, attached in some way to an alleged divine invitation or revelation. While these accounts sometimes contain painful and tragic circumstances that catalyze people's discovery of their calling, those who read and hear these accounts are left with the impression that finding one's calling ends with fulfillment, joy, and contentment. As one of our friends said with great passion, "Finally I've found the calling that I've been looking for all my life. This is what I was meant to do." Who would not want to arrive at this position in life? Although this may be the popular portrayal of calling, a shadow side needs to be acknowledged and considered. Three examples will illustrate what we mean.

Examples of the Shadow Side of Calling

The first example comes from our current political and church landscape. When she was the press secretary early in President Trump's administration, Sarah Sanders commented in an interview, "I think God calls all of us to fill different roles at different times, and I think that He wanted Donald Trump to become president, and that's why he's there."[2] We do not bring this up to make a political statement one way or the other. Rather, we point out her assumption that God works in a normative way with all (or at least some) people regarding their jobs and roles in life. What if Hillary Clinton had won the election in 2016? Would Sanders express the same sentiment, that God had called her to be president, or would Sanders avoid the use of calling language? And what about the results of the 2020 presidential election? Has God now called Joe Biden to that role? Again, would Sanders agree?

We often look to examples in the OT such as Moses when endorsing those whom we want to affirm as appointed by God. At the same time that God appointed Moses, God also hardened Pharaoh's heart and appointed him for something completely different. Are these "appointments" God's call for Moses's and Pharaoh's lives? Many Christians think so. But is this how calling works for God's people today? Is this in any way normative?

This is far more than just a squabble about semantics and definitions. Remember, words shape culture. It is laudable to empower people to find something in life that gives them passion and fulfillment, to pursue a formal ministry job, or to identify a life theme that expands beyond a job or career. Yet this has created a culture in which people may claim a calling that none can question. In 2018, the *Houston Chronicle* and *San Antonio Express-News* conducted extensive research into sexual abuse of over seven hundred victims in Southern Baptist churches by pastors and church leaders over the course of twenty years.[3] Consider the following observations, first by the article's authors and then by one of the abuse victims:

SBC churches and organizations share resources and materials, and together they fund missionary trips and seminaries. Most pastors are ordained locally after they've convinced a small group of church elders that they've been *called to service by God*. There is

2. Sullivan, "Sarah Sanders."
3. *Houston Chronicle*, "Chronicle Investigation."

no central database that tracks ordinations, or sexual abuse convictions or allegations. All of that makes Southern Baptist churches highly susceptible to predators, says Christa Brown, an activist who wrote a book about being molested as a child by a pastor at her SBC church in Farmers Branch, a Dallas suburb. "It's a perfect profession for a con artist, because all he has to do is talk a good talk and convince people that he's been *called by God*, and bingo, he gets to be a Southern Baptist minister," said Brown, who lives in Colorado. "Then he can infiltrate the entirety of the SBC, move from church to church, from state to state, go to bigger churches and more prominent churches where he has more influence and power, and it all starts in some small church."[4]

Here's the shadow side to "calling." The functional use of calling language has created a culture in which narcissists, predators, and abusers can beat the system, so to speak, and take leadership positions in our churches by claiming a divine calling. We contend that this is not the biblical meaning of calling, no matter how convincing one's claim to it may be or how popular this use of the label is. Is claiming to have God's call sufficient? How can we know if God calls someone to a specific job, task, or role? And if God does, is this sort of divine directive the exception rather than the norm? Unreflective Christians far too often and far too quickly trust someone's personal account of their "call to ministry." As authors, we do not want to diminish or deny when God clearly appoints a person for a particular job, task, or role. But rather than talk about this in terms of calling, we will see that Scripture gives us other language to use to detect and discern how God is working to direct people's lives in response to his calling.

As a second example of calling's shadow side, consider how many people entertain unrealistic expectations of how God works in their lives. Because of the way that calling language has dominated Christian discourse, people are encouraged to expect God to work in particular ways in their lives. But when they do not

4. Downen, Olsen, and Tedesco, "Abuse of Faith," emphasis added.

experience God in these specific ways, they are easily left confused, discouraged, and frustrated. With an understanding that God calls people to specific jobs, tasks, and roles, both the church's laity and those pursuing occupational church work feel this uncertainty in unique ways. As seminary professors, we have sat with countless students who exhibit this shadow side of calling. They have confessed that they lied on scholarship applications requiring them to give an account of their call to ministry. Our exchanges have followed these lines:

> Student: "So, I need to confess to you that I lied on my scholarship application. I don't have a calling to ministry, so I just made something up. Is it okay that I want to be a pastor and want to be equipped in seminary for this work? Others have affirmed my gifting and desire; that is why I am here. What do I do now since I lied?"
>
> Professor: "You do have a calling. It is to Christ, and it applies to the whole of your life. Gifting and desire are not the same as calling. Let's talk about how you can live out your calling to Christ in the whole of your life as you also discern and develop your gifting and desire for pastoral ministry."[5]

We have visibly seen the weight taken off many shoulders as they are freed from undue pressure to find the correct connection between some mystical sense of calling and a job or formal ministry position.

Unnecessary expectations are also exacerbated by the realities of the church job market. Put simply, a seminary degree does not guarantee a full-time, salaried job with health benefits in a local church upon graduation. Yet seminaries market their degree programs in a way that encourages prospective students to attend

---

5. While some would claim that desire and gifting indicate a call to ministry, we believe this is a conflation of ideas. Gifting is gifting; desire is desire; calling is calling. We must be careful not to conflate calling with other significant biblical concepts. This will be discussed in greater detail later.

so that they can find or be equipped for their "calling," which they understandably equate with a job or career. Consider the following hypothetical situation (based on several situations we have witnessed):

> A student feels or senses a "call" to be a pastor (this sense is based on the Christian culture's prevalent use of calling language). Others even affirm this pursuit. She or he is told that they need to get a master's degree to be equipped for pastoral ministry. This student enrolls in seminary and also takes on a significant part-time ministry role at a local church, combining seminary education with practical ministry experience. Over the course of three to five years, this student meets all the academic requirements and earns a degree. Yet upon graduation, this student cannot secure a full-time paid position in a local church and is left discouraged and frustrated because they must find some other means of supporting their family instead of being gainfully employed in church work. This was not how the student expected their calling to ministry to work, though. Was the student really "called"?

Who got it wrong? Was it the student who mistakenly sensed a "call to ministry" and went to seminary with certain expectations of what a call entailed? Or was it the people who affirmed this call in the first place and encouraged the student to pursue seminary education? Or did the seminary err in telling the student to pursue and be equipped for such a calling? These may not even be the right questions to ask because the real issue is not whom to blame. We contend that the real issue is an inadequate theology of calling that reveals its limitations and inadequacies when things do not go as planned or hoped for. Perhaps the seminary *did* equip the student to pursue God's calling, but that calling is not a job or ministry.

This does not only apply to seminary students looking for a job. What about the pastors who have been wrongfully let go by unhealthy and dysfunctional church boards—did their calling leave them, was it revoked, or was it something else altogether? What about the pastors who hang on to their job far too long or are allowed to remain in their role because they insist on their calling to that particular position? Does a pastor's sense of calling justify such actions or even incompetence? What if a church needs to close its doors, for whatever reason, and the pastor must find a job in business or the nonprofit world to make ends meet for the family? Does God suspend someone's call for a time or even terminate it? Can a calling go away for a season? Must the pastor wait for God to issue a new call? We have heard many use language about "God's timing" when discussing calling. When circumstances seem desirable, God's timing is perfect. When things do not go as planned, we must wait on God's timing. Does God's call start on a specific date? How does one know when God issues it? We must be careful not to invoke "God's timing" when it fits our definitions or is convenient for our agendas and disregard it when it is not. There are many other scenarios that we could include here, but these illustrate that unnecessary expectations easily follow when we attach calling to a professional ministry position or job.

It is not just seminary students or pastors who experience this shadow side of calling. Unreasonable expectations about calling trouble many average church people as well. Often these take two different forms. First, there is a value divide that exists within the body of Christ. Those who are "called" typically pursue some form of explicit ministry work such as pastors, missionaries, Christian educators, and Christian nonprofit workers. We use the phrase "vocational Christian ministry." Everyone else's "ministry" is functionally of lesser value (though we would never admit this) and serves to support these specially called ones. Ministry for layfolk is often limited in scope to volunteer opportunities within a local church program, such as helping out in the youth group, singing on the worship team, hosting a small group, going on a short-term mission trip, or greeting visitors on Sunday mornings.

Perhaps they work in parachurch ministries or in other nonprofit organizations as paid workers or volunteers. We do not wish to diminish the importance of these roles and responsibilities, but why is calling language not used for these tasks, and should it be? What does "calling" mean for laypeople? Can one be "called" to a secular job? These questions are important but confusing.

The second troubling feature of calling discourse results from widespread efforts to validate everyone's daily work as a vocation or calling. As we will see, this push is not a recent phenomenon in the history of the church but has gained significant momentum in recent years. The current iteration of the Faith at Work Movement has leveraged a notion of calling to inspire people to find deeper significance and meaning in their daily work, connecting Sunday to Monday, so to speak.[6] Convinced of God's kingdom work in the world outside of formal church ministries and programs, those not working in churches are encouraged to see their jobs as a calling. The motivation behind this may be right and even appropriate for some people, but this initiative also has significant drawbacks. The same expectations and complications that pastors experience about calling are now being felt by those in the business world.

One of us has a friend who was trying to connect the dots between her faith and her job. "I don't have a calling!" she insisted multiple times. Despite my protests, she had been so influenced by the popular notions of calling, especially as it relates to work, that she held herself accountable to unhealthy expectations. She could not detach herself from the expectation that every Christian needs to be able to identify a particular calling related to their gainful employment.

6. The "faith at work movement" is "a loose global network of scholars, clergy, students, and marketplace leaders" seeking to encourage and equip "Christians to see their work as part of God's purposes in and for the world. . . . Today, hundreds of highly effective faith at work organizations serve individual Christians, companies, denominations, parachurch organizations, colleges and universities, and a broad spectrum of churches." https://spu.edu/depts/uc/response/new/2012-autumn/features/faith-at-work-movement.asp.

Her story raises some important questions about a person's daily work and the issue of calling. Should people experience angst because they have never sensed a calling from God? What about those who work in jobs they feel are meaningless or mundane? What if one must settle for a job below one's qualifications and experience? Are such jobs nonetheless their calling? Or have they missed their calling? How does the popular understanding of calling fit those who find themselves in an unhealthy or unethical work environment, or those who work in a job not because they want to but because it provides the bare necessities of life for them and their dependents? How does calling fit in?

How does a popular understanding of calling function in today's constantly changing workforce environment? Entire industries are going away, replaced by a gig economy, where people work multiple short-term contracted jobs. The increasing cost of living outstrips wages, requiring people to work multiple jobs to make ends meet, and a degree (including a seminary degree) or a union certification does not guarantee a job in one's desired field. We fully affirm the value and dignity of people's work as a means of bringing God's kingdom to earth as it is in heaven, but using calling terminology in this way may be more detrimental than helpful and does not seem to work well in many contexts. We contend that this reflects a misunderstanding of the word "calling."

As a final example of the shadow side of calling, consider how popular discourse on the subject has been used to manipulate people. "Calling" has developed into a powerful concept, and therefore the term itself carries much weight. Apart from the name of Jesus Christ, there may not be a word that has more power than "calling" to alter the course of someone's life. People have quit jobs, pursued new careers, moved their families to the other side of the world, and initiated other dramatic life changes because of a sense of calling. People in positions of power and influence, whether in organizations or in personal relationships, can misuse calling language to further their own agendas. Words shape culture, and that culture is the landscape of people's lives.

As an example, listen to Katie's story. Katie graduated from a prominent seminary here in the United States, prepared to serve God in some capacity. While in seminary she was told through missions initiatives, "Unless you are specifically called to stay, you are called to go overseas." Notice the language that was employed to define the default calling for a committed Christian. Because of the huge need for missionaries in other lands, calling language is employed to recruit people for missionary service. Because Katie did not sense a "calling to stay" (note how subjective this becomes), and despite an actual lack of desire to go, she headed overseas to work with an organization in a Middle Eastern country. Sadly, she was led by dysfunctional and unhealthy leaders in that country, worked alongside ill-equipped and immature team members, and admittedly—as a young, single, white female in a Middle Eastern country—was ill-equipped herself for the work in front of her. It was a hard experience on several levels. As she looks back on her time in seminary, what sticks out the most is how the calling language was used alongside promotional videos to portray a glamorous, compelling, and spiritually fulfilling life overseas that proved to be the antithesis of her experience. She spent three years in the Middle East and is now living in the Denver area, doing good work as a therapist and leaving her supposed overseas calling in the past.

What is most tragic is not that Katie had rough experiences, but rather that these rough experiences were attached to "calling" in a way that was quite manipulative. Well-meaning missions recruiters used and glamorized calling language to elicit a particular response. Some may have served successfully across the globe because of this missionary emphasis. But because of the Christian culture's use of calling language, Katie's story serves as a warning about its power to change lives, and not always for the better. We need a deeper dive into our use of calling terminology to found it on a robust biblical and theological exploration of the topic. The goal is not merely to make sure our definitions are accurate but also to recognize and enable God's people to faithfully engage the needs of the world in whatever context they find themselves. In addition, and perhaps especially, God's people must be equipped to do so when the varied contexts of their lives shift and change.

Now that we have considered the shadow side of the popular use of calling terminology, let us take a closer look at two elements that compose this functional theology, though some of this has been implicit in what we have just covered. First, we will identify the primary target audiences of calling terminology as it is commonly used. Second, we will examine the primary features of the resources that have promoted the popular understanding of calling terminology.[7]

Target Audiences

In the past twenty years alone, around ninety books have been published with "call/calling/called" in the title or subtitle.[8] There are also countless other books that address calling at a subsidiary level. In addition to these books, many blogs, sermons, articles, and conferences add their voices to the calling conversation. These calling resources target three different audiences.

First, calling language regularly singles out pastors and those pursuing some form of Christian leadership.[9] These resources

7. Because our findings extend beyond published books to include other media such as blogs, sermons, podcasts, and articles, we will use the term "resource" to refer to the broad corpus that mentions and discusses the topic of calling.

8. There may be more than ninety published books; these are only the ones we discovered. Our list includes some that have been self-published, but because they are available through online stores such as Amazon.com and can contribute to shaping our culture's broader understanding of calling, we include them along with books published by a commercial press. Most of these books are written from a religious perspective, but others speak of calling from a purely secular perspective.

9. Examples include Allen, *Discerning Your Call*; Harvey, *Am I Called?*; Milton, *Called?*; Padilla, *Now That I'm Called*; and Tripp, *Dangerous Calling*.

often target either men or women, depending on which side of the gender-role conversation one falls.[10] While some resources attempt an explanation and definition of what calling is, others simply assume a commonly understood working knowledge of calling (which is part of the problem we are addressing).

Second, a number of calling resources target all other Christians, emphasizing how calling relates to their lives despite the fact that they are not pursuing professional ministry roles.[11] Within this group of resources, authors focus on specific audiences, such as the aging, the retired, and those who work.[12]

Religious folk are not alone in employing calling terminology. A *third* target audience we have observed extends beyond those who would attach calling to God as the Caller. The book *Masters of Craft: Old Jobs in the New Urban Economy* is a sociologist's inquiry into why young professionals are leaving corporate jobs and pursuing a living in jobs such as whole-animal butchers, high-end barbers, cocktail crafters, and brewers. Ocejo makes the following observation as to why people are making these career changes: "The jobs in this book have been recoded as 'cool,' creative ones, with opportunities for young workers to shape tastes, innovate, and achieve higher status. They seek out these jobs as careers instead of other jobs in the new economy with higher profiles. For them, these jobs are vocations, or callings, providing meaning through materially oriented, craft-based manual labor, in front of knowing peers and an accepting public."[13] Although he is not writing from or endorsing a Christian view of calling, Ocejo identifies a significant underlying issue also at

10. Tripp's *Dangerous Calling* and Harvey's *Am I Called?* are explicitly directed to a male audience; Padilla's *Now That I'm Called* is directed toward women pursuing teaching and preaching roles.

11. Examples include Guinness, *The Call*; Labberton, *Called*; Wilson, *More*.

12. Examples include Keller and Alsdorf, *Every Good Endeavor*; Nelson, *Work Matters*; Raynor, *Called to Create*; Sherman, *Kingdom Calling*; G. Smith, *Courage & Calling*; Stevens, *Aging Matters*; Stevens, *The Other Six Days*; and Ward, *I Am a Leader*.

13. Ocejo, *Masters of Craft*, 18.

play with Christians and their use of calling terminology. The broader and adopted use of this term may be fueled by an inability or unwillingness to find significance in some divine connection, but instead to seek meaning in tangible jobs, tasks, and roles.

Ocejo's observations about calling parallel the way calling language is used in Jessica Huie's *Purpose: Find Your Truth and Embrace Your Calling*. Motivated by her own life story, Huie encourages her readers to find a deeper meaning and purpose for their lives. Rather than living a self-focused life, she urges, identifying and following one's calling helps a person see beyond themselves, which in turn leads to a more fulfilling life.[14] Although she does acknowledge that this deeper sense of purpose and meaning is associated with a universal power, God, Spirit, or source,[15] Huie's view of calling is completely subjective. Each person must define and make meaning for themselves.

In a similar way, Dave Isay's *Callings: The Purpose and Passion of Work* attaches calling to a sense of purpose and meaning found in one's daily work. Using his own story as a foundation, Isay describes calling as "what I was going to do for the rest of my life."[16] He affirms Studs Terkel's observation that work is about the search "for daily meaning as well as daily bread, for recognition as well as cash, for astonishment rather than torpor; in short, for a sort of life rather than a Monday through Friday sort of dying."[17] The accounts of people's work in Isay's book are "proof of Terkel's proposition."[18] Ultimately for Isay, calling is about finding meaning in one's work while being driven by an inner voice; calling is something that needs to be found.

Having briefly considered these three targeted audiences, we can now set forth the patterns for how calling language is used.

14. See esp. chaps. 2–3.
15. Huie, *Purpose*, 25.
16. Isay, *Callings*, 2.
17. Isay, *Callings*, 3, quoting Terkel, *Working*, xi.
18. Isay, *Callings*, 3.

Primary Features Associated with Popular Calling Language

1. Calling Is to a Job, Task, or Role

This first common feature found within popular calling discourse surfaced in our previous observations about calling's shadow side. A myriad of resources address jobs, tasks, and roles related to occupational church or religious ministry. But it is not just professional ministry jobs and roles that many calling resources emphasize. Within this job-, task-, and role-orientation toward calling, we need to address the relationship between calling and vocation. These two terms are often used interchangeably, and understandably so. The calling language in the NT comes from the Greek words *klēsis* (calling), *klētos* ([the] called), and *kaleō* ([I] call). Vocation comes from the Latin words *vox*, *vocare*, and *vocatio*, which mean "voice," "to call," and "summons." Today, when most people talk about their vocation, they typically refer to their gainful employment. Some, though, use this term to refer to certain types of work that are considered to be more spiritual or service-oriented in nature. Others refer to trade-industry jobs as vocations. Along with that, there is a trend within the Faith at Work Movement to reclaim a vision of vocation that applies to all of life. It can be confusing to know what different people actually mean when using the term "vocation" because, like "calling," there is a wide range of meanings in current use. Are they synonyms in some uses, but not in others?

Historically, we can credit Martin Luther and other Reformers for this emphasis on one's occupation as a vocation.[19] Luther especially was pushing back against a divide between the sacred work done by priests and monks (and other religious persons) and the seemingly less important work done by everyone else. Using the idea of vocation, Luther sought to elevate the work of those such as blacksmiths, bakers, farmers, and miners because, he argued,

---

19. In chap. 2 we will take a longer look at the historical development of a Christian view of calling and then critique Luther more thoroughly in chap. 5.

that was the station in life to which God had called them. Luther's emphasis on the sacred nature of ordinary work is an important feature of the Reformation. However, we will show that Luther's connecting vocation and work has led to a misunderstanding of the nature of God's calling in the whole of our lives. While many take great pains to expand the view of vocation and calling beyond jobs, they still far too easily equate calling with jobs, tasks, and roles.

We can illustrate this by addressing how calling comes up in some job interviews for faith-based work. Let us assume the common view that God calls people to specific ministry positions. What would you say if you were asked in the final interview for an incredible ministry opportunity, "Is God calling you to this job?" If you answer "Yes," does that mean the interview process is over and the job is yours? If God has called you, what more needs to be said? Why would anyone dare to question God's calling? If you answer "No" or "I'm not sure," does that also mean the interview process is over and you should look for another job? Why should they hire you if you cannot affirm that God has called you to the job? Is there no correct answer? Or does the problem grow out of the confusion about what the term "calling" means?

Here's another example. Upon graduating from seminary, Luke took a job with Fellowship of Christian Athletes (FCA), working as a missionary in the Dominican Republic. His work focused primarily on baseball ministry to young men pursuing a professional baseball career. After a year and a half or so in the Dominican Republic, an opportunity arose for Luke and his family to move to Florida so that he could work as the director of operations for a small nonprofit called Man Up and Go. After a year in that job, because of his connections in the baseball world, Luke was approached to consider a job overseeing the chaplains for all major league baseball teams that go to Florida for spring training (Red Sox, Phillies, Orioles, etc.). While discussing this opportunity,

Luke shared both the pros and cons of taking such a job and the pros and cons of staying in his job with Man Up and Go. For anyone who loves baseball, the decision would have been a no-brainer, but Luke was not starstruck by professional ballplayers and was wrestling through some significant competing factors in this decision.

During his final job interview for this head chaplain role, he was asked, "Is God calling you to this job?" What do you imagine the interviewers were asking? Here is a summary of his answer: "No, God is not calling me to this job. My calling is to Christ. I am actually a husband and a father before I am a chaplain. I feel compelled and gifted to disciple men, and this job allows me the opportunity to do that work no differently than my work with FCA and Man Up and Go." Though Luke denied being called to this job, that denial did not deter the interviewers from offering it to him, and he accepted. But what might have happened if the interviewers were hung up on Luke's denial of a specific call to that job? Fortunately, Luke enlarged his interviewers' understanding of what "calling" entailed.

Both of these scenarios pinpoint a problem with the popular understanding of calling. Rather than worry about picking the one job or even type of work that God is supposedly calling us to, we may simply seek opportunities to be faithful in whatever we do. More on this below.

2. Calling Is Individualized and Specific

Second, calling language is often used in a very individualized and specific manner. While we may at times hear people refer to our collective calling, most often the use of calling language is quite individualistic. Consider these recent book titles: *More: Find Your Personal Calling and Live Life to the Fullest Measure*; *A Higher Calling: Claiming God's Best for Your Life*; *Aging Matters: Finding Your Calling for the Rest of Your Life*; *Embracing Your Second Calling: Find Passion and Purpose for the Rest of*

Your Life; and *Courage & Calling: Embracing Your God-Given Potential.*[20] We readily recognize the individualistic nature of our culture. Sadly, however, this cultural lens has shaped our use of the word "calling." Having "my own calling" from God sounds very affirming and alluring.

Beyond just the book titles listed above, there is an oft-quoted statement from Frederick Buechner that needs careful inspection: "The place God calls you to is the place where your deep gladness and the world's deep hunger meet."[21] Reading what comes right before this statement provides more insight into what Buechner is really getting at:

> There are all different kinds of voices calling you to all different kinds of work, and the problem is to find out which is the voice of God rather than of Society, say, or the Super-ego, or Self-Interest. By and large a good rule for finding out is this. The kind of work God usually calls you to is the kind of work (*a*) that you need most to do and (*b*) that the world most needs to have done. If you really get a kick out of your work, you've presumably met requirement (*a*), but if your work is writing TV deodorant commercials, the chances are you've missed requirement (*b*). On the other hand, if your work is being a doctor in a leper colony, you have probably met requirement (*b*), but if most of the time you're bored and depressed by it, the chances are you have not only bypassed (*a*) but probably aren't helping your patients much either. . . . The place God calls you to is the place where your deep gladness and the world's deep hunger meet.[22]

It is understandable why Buechner's statement is often quoted, but its use reflects our culture's individualistic conditioning and our desire to do something great in life and not a truly biblical

20. Wilson, *More*; Thomas, *Higher Calling*; Stevens, *Aging Matters*; Bourke, *Embracing Your Second Calling*; and G. Smith, *Courage & Calling*.
21. Buechner, *Wishful Thinking*, 95.
22. Buechner, *Wishful Thinking*, 95.

understanding of calling. Unintentionally, Buechner has done four unfortunate things: (1) reinforced a significance divide that already exists within our culture, whereby a person's significance and worth are determined by the sort of work that they do; (2) declared certain sorts of work to be worthy of God's leading and others not; (3) emphasized that it is primarily in our gainfully employed work that we can live out God's calling; and (4) taught that faithfulness is conditioned by personal gladness.

David Brooks echoes a similar sentiment when he writes that finding a vocation is about asking, "What will touch my deepest desire? What activity gives me my deepest satisfaction? Second, it's about fit. . . . It's about finding a match between a delicious activity and a social need."[23] This is not to say that a person should not pursue jobs and opportunities that bring a deep sense of gladness and a congruence between their desires and the world's significant hungers if they have the opportunity to do so. But this is scarcely realistic for many if not most of God's people around the globe. It sounds rather elitist. And, most important, it is not what the Bible means by God's call on a person's life.

What do we say to those experiencing homelessness in our community, refugees, the unemployed, those in and recently released from prison, the retired, and those working jobs that do not bring delight but simply put food on the table and a roof over their heads? Are they filling a great need as Buechner or Brooks envision it? Are they experiencing great delight in what they do? And more pointedly for our purposes: Is there a theology of calling that can apply to Christians in these circumstances?

We think that a correct theology of calling can and will apply to all Christians, but not so the all-too-popular individualized understanding. Or better yet, we contend that a more faithful theology of calling will help direct the shape of a believer's life no matter what their current status or circumstances. Put still

23. Brooks, *Second Mountain*, 121–22.

another way, we contend that a theology of calling that is truly faithful to Scripture and not just pious language *must* apply to all Christians at all times and in all places. An overly individualized and specific view of calling as popularly presented just does not work. It ends up limiting more than it liberates.

As we will seek to demonstrate, there is an individualized aspect of calling, but in the Scriptures, calling is corporate before it is individual. God calls individuals to be a certain sort of people rather than to engage in specific tasks, roles, and jobs.

3. Calling Is Multiple

Third, calling language is often used in the plural: callings or vocations. A couple of book titles reflect this: *Callings: Following and Finding an Authentic Life*; and *Vocation: Discerning Our Callings in Life*.[24] Where does this idea of having multiple callings come from? Historically and theologically, some Christians have distinguished between the general and specific callings of God's people: the general calling is to salvation, and the specific callings are to particular forms of work or activity.[25] In recent years, some have relabeled the general and specific distinction as primary and secondary callings. Os Guinness has become a seminal voice on this point. He emphasized primary and secondary callings in his popular book *The Call*, and this language has been adopted by many others. Tom Nelson observes, "Guinness has given considerable thought to a robust theology of vocation. Keeping the gospel central, Os makes a helpful distinction between our primary calling and our secondary callings. He rightly points out that Scripture first and foremost emphasizes our primary calling to Christ. . . . But Os also insightfully points out that each one of us has also been given a secondary calling, and an essential aspect of this

---

24. Levoy, *Callings*; Schuurman, *Vocation*.
25. There is also a theological distinction between the general and specific call that is efficacious for salvation, but that theological discussion is beyond the scope of this book.

particular calling is to do a specific work."[26] Recall our previous observations about the individualization and specification of calling, which here is enlarged to multiple callings.

Although Nelson alleges that Guinness has given us "a robust theology of vocation," when reading *The Call* one is hard-pressed to find a biblical argument for calling, let alone a robust theology of calling or vocation. While Guinness rightly emphasizes the role of the Caller for our calling and acknowledges the semantic range of meaning for calling terminology in the Bible, biblical arguments for his primary/secondary distinction are noticeably lacking. Guinness relies on narrative texts in the Bible rather than didactic uses of calling language by the biblical authors. The only passage he cites from Paul is Col. 3:23, which does not even deal with calling directly. Rather than "a robust theology of vocation," Guinness admits that the chapters in his book "are not academic or theoretical; they have been hammered out on the anvil of my own experience."[27] Guinness's primary/secondary categorization may help him understand and communicate the experiences and phenomena of his own life, but his subjective categorization is not helpful for those who cannot identify with his experiences, and it cannot be used to devise a normative theology of calling, which must be based on biblical exegesis.[28]

4. Calling Is Hidden

A fourth calling feature regularly employed alleges that one's calling is hidden and must be (often) arduously discovered. Calling is often expressed in the following ways: "Find your calling,"

---

26. Nelson, *Work Matters*, 16.
27. Guinness, *The Call*, 6.
28. We have not yet arrived at the exegetical portion of the book, but we want to provide a hermeneutical observation. The way we refer to calling and callings suggests that they are a thing or object. In other words, we consider "calling" a noun. When calling language is used as a noun in the NT, however, it is always in the singular. Along with this, when calling language is used adjectivally, it specifies something of our identity. We will explore this in chap. 3 when we do a more thorough biblical study of calling in Scripture.

"discover your calling," or "uncover your calling." Numerous books carry this sentiment: *Purpose: Find Your Truth and Embrace Your Calling*; *The Soul's Code: In Search of Character and Calling*; *More: Find Your Personal Calling and Live Life to the Fullest Measure*;[29] and more. *Relevant Magazine* published an online article titled "How to Find Your Calling (and Why Most People Get This Wrong)."[30] Forbes.com has an article titled "20 Ways to Find Your Calling."[31] Mindbodygreen.com has an article titled "10 Strategies for Gradually Figuring Out Your 'Life's Calling.'"[32] Our goal here is not to unpack what each of these says about the nature of calling (though most are geared toward a personal sense of purpose, passion, and talent related to a job, task, or role), but rather simply to highlight the assumption that one's calling is hidden, lost, or kept as a secret from us. One of these calling resources even goes so far as to compare finding one's calling to finding a needle in a haystack.[33]

Mark this: every time a Christian confidently describes finding a personal sense of calling regarding some pursuit in life (or the job or career field they are going into, or their life's purpose or theme), many other Christians wonder whether or not they have true significance or worth in God's kingdom work in the world because they have not experienced the same sense of clarity or revelation. Why haven't they found their calling? Are they just not looking hard enough or in the right places? Or is this simply a misguided pursuit? We do propose to help people find their calling, but we will argue that if someone is in Christ, their calling has already been revealed by God in his Word. The NT clearly articulates the nature of a Christian's calling. Our calling is not hidden. We will argue that the issue is not how to find some hidden or esoteric calling; the issue is whether or not we are willing

29. Huie, *Purpose*; Wilson, *More*; Hillman, *Soul's Code*.
30. Goins, "How to Find Your Calling."
31. Hagy, "20 Ways to Find Your Calling."
32. Ottaway, "10 Strategies."
33. Wilson, *More*, 28–29.

to accept our already revealed calling and then, in Christ, to live out that calling in the whole of our lives.

Most likely, what people often label as "a calling from God" may in fact be a subjective affirmation of a fortuitous set of circumstances, or the expression of one's gifting, or a baptized and spiritualized (for religious people) personal desire—whether honorable or not—or simply a decision that is the result of wisdom and discernment. What if Christians already have everything they need for a godly life, being in Christ (2 Pet. 1:3)?[34] What if we were to put more emphasis on walking by faith and practicing discernment as we confront the various decisions we need to make in life, both big and small? What if we stopped trying to find or wait for the burning bush or the blinding light or the booming (or still, small) voice from heaven? What if those sorts of dramatic events are actually fewer and rarer than many writers and speakers admit and are not really intended to be normative? And what if we have no evidence or reason to confirm that Noah, Abraham, Moses, Rahab, Esther, Ruth, Isaiah, Jeremiah, Ezekiel, Daniel, Paul, and others searched for a hidden calling? Perhaps their unique and specifically appointed role in God's redemptive story found them. More on that below.

Often Christians who claim to have "found their calling" are referring to some sort of pastoral or missionary work or to some noble humanitarian effort. We will argue that calling more accurately reflects how one *redemptively* engages the mundane, ordinary things of life. Remember Buechner's critical statement about the person who works to produce deodorant TV commercials. What if you are a Christian who is a marketing expert and has an opportunity to pitch an idea to Old Spice for their next clever ad campaign? In Buechner's view, apparently, that cannot be a calling. Must that person accept a life devoid of a calling? Or find it somewhere else?

34. The passage in 2 Pet. 1:3 merits repeating in full: "His divine power has given us everything we need for a godly life through our knowledge of him who called us by his own glory and goodness" (NIV).

In *Desiring the Kingdom*, James K. A. Smith comments on the influence that product-marketing campaigns have on shaping our culture at large because of our bent toward consumerism.[35] Rather than discourage a Christian from working as part of a marketing campaign for a deodorant brand, can't we affirm marketing experts who are empowered and equipped by the church to view their work in a redemptive way, somehow engaging the needs of the world even through developing deodorant commercials? We do not pretend here to know what that would look like, but we trust that a marketing expert who is in Christ, empowered by the Holy Spirit, and sent out by the church can brainstorm and imagine the redemptive possibilities in the context of their work since they know their work better than we do. We believe we should give them permission to do it as a reflection of their calling to Christ. But to accomplish this, the church needs a more robust and biblically based understanding of calling.

5. Calling Is to a Person—Christ

The final feature in our survey of the prevalent uses of calling is the Christian's calling to Christ.[36] There are several books that mention this calling, often assuming it as a given and then focusing on one or more of the above-mentioned ways of using calling terminology. Dave Harvey summarizes it this way: "We assume the gospel, and then dedicate ourselves more to the special call of ministry."[37] In these instances, the Christian's calling to Christ functionally takes a back seat so that "more important" discussion can take place regarding "how to find one's calling" or "engage one's secondary callings." There are, however, some who emphasize this calling to Christ. We will highlight three—Lesslie

35. J. Smith, *Desiring the Kingdom*, 75–77.
36. The previous four calling features are found throughout calling resources produced in the last twenty years; this final feature is used far less frequently as a point of emphasis and extended reflection; thus we draw from resources that go back further than twenty years.
37. Harvey, *Am I Called?*, 38.

Newbigin, Gordon Smith, and Ray Anderson—and then return to them in chapter 5. Newbigin was a British missionary to India in the middle of the twentieth century. He wrote about the transition that Christianity was experiencing, going from a majority religious view to a minority perspective within an increasingly pluralistic world. Ever a churchman, Newbigin presented ways in which the body of Christ should be equipped for ministry in the public spaces of society. He believed the church was to be God's presence in and to the world: "What God has given to the world in Christ is something different, an actual divine humanity, a real presence of God in human history, not a new idea about God, but God made man, and calling men into fellowship with Himself."[38] God accomplishes his saving purpose by calling people to himself and sending them into the world.[39] Newbigin refers to calling as God bringing the church into existence through Christ, which follows the pattern of how he called Israel to be his people.[40]

In his *Truth to Tell*, Newbigin further describes what it means for God's people to fulfill their calling—to be sent into the world:

> But the local Christian congregation, where the word of the gospel is preached, where in the sacrament of the Eucharist we are united with Christ in his dying for the sin of the world and in his risen life for the sake of the world, is the place where we are enabled to develop a shared life in which sin can be both recognized and forgiven. If this congregation understands its true character as a holy priesthood for the sake of the world, and if its members are equipped for the exercise of that priesthood in their secular employments, then there is a point of growth for a new social order.[41]

38. Newbigin, *Household of God*, 56–57.
39. Newbigin, *Household of God*, 62–63.
40. Newbigin, *Household of God*, 48–50.
41. Newbigin, *Truth to Tell*, 86–87.

The church is responsible for equipping God's people to do the work of ministry as those called to be God's people. He uses the metaphor of "undercover agents" to describe how Christians should view themselves in the public spaces of society.[42] They are to engage the world, equipped by the church "for active and informed participation in public life in such a way that the Christian faith shapes that participation."[43] In this way for Newbigin, calling relates to how God forms the church and *not* to how he appoints individual Christians to particular types of work.

Similarly, Ray Anderson understands calling in relationship to the church. Anderson was a farmer-turned-pastor-turned-professor. His own life story and career arc are directly tied to his understanding of the direction of one's calling and vocation. Luther understood vocation only in terms of the earthly kingdom: vocation was not directed heavenward, but only earthward. Anderson sees things the other way around. While being quite concrete in the way he reflects theologically, Anderson believes the Christian's calling is to Christ rather than to a definite field of activity on earth. The Christian is called to participate in the ongoing ministry of Christ: "The ongoing ministry of Jesus Christ gives both content and direction to the Church in its ministry. Jesus is the minister *par excellence*. He ministers to the Father for the sake of the world. . . . The church has no existence apart from being called into being through this ministry and equipped for it by the gift of the Holy Spirit."[44] In this way, baptism is every believer's entry point, or calling, to ministry: "There is a sense in which one can say that baptism into Christ is ordination into the ministry of Christ. As Christ was called and ordained to His Messianic ministry through baptism, so the baptism of every person can be viewed as a calling into the ministry of Christ. The special ordination that sets baptized persons apart as representatives of

42. Newbigin, *Truth to Tell*, 83.
43. Newbigin, *Truth to Tell*, 81.
44. Anderson, "Theology for Ministry," 8.

the ministry of Christ through the church is still grounded upon baptism."[45] Anderson's contribution to our conversation not only extends to the calling of the church's laity but also provides a different way of understanding a pastor's calling to ministry. Although Anderson does affirm the pastor's calling into ministry, he sees this in terms of being sent rather than being called. He writes, "Let me present another way of looking at the concept of a call to ministry and to a church. Strictly speaking the calling of a minister is to participate in Christ's calling to serve the Father and, secondarily, to go where one is sent, as did Jesus."[46] By understanding the direction of calling in this way, and by not seeing the location of one's calling as being on earth, a pastor does not need to bear the responsibility of meeting every single need within the ministry, because it is not their ministry but Christ's.

Gordon Smith is our final example of someone who primarily looks at calling through the lens of participation in Christ. In *Called to Be Saints*, Smith presents a theology of Christian maturity. According to Smith, anemic views of Christian maturity abound today, and he proposes that "what is needed is a theological vision of the human vocation—something with nuance and substance, an articulation of the Christian life that is congruent with the New Testament call to faith in Christ."[47] He makes a specific connection between our calling to Christ and Christian maturity, as described in 2 Peter, where we "are reminded that new birth is not an end but a beginning; our election or calling in Christ and to Christ is for a particular purpose—maturity in Christ."[48]

Smith's articulation of spiritual maturity is rooted in trinitarian theology: "The call to holiness comes from the Father as an

---

45. Anderson, *Soul of Ministry*, 84. We will revisit this idea in chap. 5 when we develop a theology of calling.

46. Anderson, *Soul of Ministry*, 85.

47. G. Smith, *Called to Be Saints*, 16.

48. G. Smith, *Called to Be Saints*, 20.

invitation to participate in the life of Christ Jesus and to do so in radical dependence on the grace of the Spirit."[49] This invitation directly ties together God's intent for humanity's creation, the reality of sin, and our redemption in Christ. Although clearly trinitarian in perspective, there is a christological emphasis in Smith's argument.[50] One of the most important implications of Smith's argument is that viewing Christian calling in this way adequately addresses all the dimensions of life: in particular, the ordinary, the mundane suffering, failure, disappointment, and pain.[51] As a result of the Christian's call in Christ to maturity and holiness, Smith proposes four specific invitations for a holy person: wisdom, doing good work, loving others in a manner consistent with how God has loved us, and happiness.[52]

Hermeneutics Employed within Calling Resources

Having surveyed these five common uses of calling terminology in contemporary resources, we deem it important to assess the popular hermeneutical methods employed by Christian writers, particularly those whose troublesome views (1–4 above) have led to the downsides described above. How do these writers employ Scripture in arriving at their understandings of calling? Exposing the popular hermeneutical strategies is crucial before we engage in our own biblical study of calling in chapter 3. Rather than return to each source we surveyed, we will attempt some broad observations on recurring features. Not all writers or contributors engage in all these tactics, but some obvious interpretive methods emerge that we must scrutinize because we believe they have unfortunate outcomes.

---

49. G. Smith, *Called to Be Saints*, 25.
50. See G. Smith, *Called to Be Saints*, chap. 2, "Union with Christ: The Essence of the Christian Life."
51. G. Smith, *Called to Be Saints*, 30.
52. G. Smith, *Called to Be Saints*, 36. He expands each of these invitations in later chapters.

First, we find that writers often use OT and NT narratives of prominent biblical characters to substantiate popular views of calling. These stories are selectively chosen and often emphasize individuals who accomplished something great for God. The stories of Abraham, Moses, Jacob, David, Esther, Nehemiah, Paul, and Jesus's disciples, for example, regularly appear in support of how God calls individuals to specific jobs, tasks, and roles.[53]

We contend that very often these popular writers start with their own assumptions about calling and then proceed to mine the Bible for examples to illustrate their understanding. They may assume that "calling" refers to a religious vocation or a secular job or that Christians must seek their own individual calling, one that uniquely fits how God made them. If they use the Scriptures at all (and many do not, as Os Guinness confessed above), they proceed to identify examples that support their presuppositions. They imply that since God called these individuals who lived important and fulfilling lives in God's service, God has a similar calling for each of us. It never occurs to them to ask whether the Scriptures intend these examples as normative for all Christians.

Further, they imply that God will call you in a way that is similar to how God called these biblical heroes. Christians are therefore encouraged to look for the equivalent of burning bushes, lights and voices, dreams and visions, or a still small voice for evidence that God is calling them. They commit the hermeneutical fallacy of viewing narratives as normative. If we recognize that although God judged Ananias and Sapphira with immediate death due to their duplicity (Acts 5:1–10), such a divine response is not normative for all liars, we must also conclude that Paul's vision of a Macedonian (Acts 16:9–10) does not prescribe how God will call others to a particular field of ministry. The same applies to

---

53. For example, Guinness, *The Call*, 63–64; Milton, *Called?*, 26; Padilla, *Now That I'm Called*, chaps. 3–4; Ward, *I Am a Leader*, 28–31.

accounts of other biblical luminaries who experienced some special "call" from God. Interpreting narratives in the Bible requires special care.[54] We must distinguish between what is descriptive and what is normative in biblical narratives.

Second, some writers correctly acknowledge the multiple uses of calling terminology in Scripture but then commit a fallacy. "Call" can be used to describe several different phenomena. For example, God *called* the light day and the darkness night in Gen. 1, God *called* out to Samuel, Jesus *called* the disciples to follow him, and Paul refers numerous times to the Christian's *call* to holiness and other Christlike characteristics. While modern authors may acknowledge the semantic range of calling terminology, they often isolate and emphasize the uses of calling terminology that fit their particular argument without sufficient regard for the contexts in which these various senses of call occur. One cannot simply take the meaning a word has in one location and import it into other contexts that are not similar. We address this fallacy more directly in chapter 4.

Our third hermeneutical observation concerns the corporate and individual nature of calling. Some resources acknowledge our common calling to Christ for salvation (though many do not) but then focus primarily on calling in an individualistic manner (as described above). But what is primary and what is secondary in our understanding of calling? Many resources start by emphasizing (or even limiting their study to) the individual nature of calling and then proceed (if at all) to address the corporate nature of calling. This order simply reinforces the predominant, culturally influenced understanding of calling that focuses on individuals. As we will show, we believe that the corporate nature of calling needs to be our starting point. We must begin with our common calling to Christ before we seek to understand the individual

54. For further insight in interpreting narratives, see W. Klein, Blomberg, and Hubbard, *Introduction to Biblical Interpretation*, 420–33 (for the OT) and 538–40 (for Acts).

nature of calling. This aligns with the ways Scripture presents the matter.

Fourth, we find a lot of what we call "concept conflation." Without warrant, calling is often equated with gifting, desire, discernment, personal purpose, and affirmation from others. For example, when discussing people's work, R. Paul Stevens comments, "Our ordinary occupations find their true meaning in something larger than personal fulfillment. They are *callings* taken up in what the apostle Paul calls 'my purpose' (2 Tim. 3:10)."[55] Yet the term "calling" does not appear at all in the passage that Stevens cites. When discussing a skilled task that one performs in their work, Stevens without warrant equates calling with what Paul refers to as his purpose. When we commit concept conflation, not only do we misunderstand and misappropriate the true nature of calling but we also fail to understand and apply correctly other biblical concepts such as gifting, desire, discernment, and affirmation from others. They receive short shrift by being subsumed under or confused with calling.

Our final hermeneutical critique concerns how Scripture is often *not* used in popular writings on calling. Many of the current resources that address calling base their claims on personal experience, either their own or that of some Christian luminary. The highly subjective nature of current calling discourse risks muddying the question of authority and normativity. Are individual experiences necessarily authoritative beyond the person having that experience? Asked differently, on what basis can I claim that my experience is normative for others? As we have demonstrated in this chapter, subjective personal experiences of calling often do not align with others' experiences and the ways various authors use calling terminology. We do not deny that personal experiences should be included in a robust understanding of calling. But rather than simply assuming that any individual

---

55. Stevens, *The Other Six Days*, 72, emphasis original.

experience is normative (and that it is a call), we need to assess personal experiences in light of careful biblical analyses and theological conversations.

Conclusion

Having surveyed the current landscape of calling, we have found that people use calling terminology in a bewildering variety of ways. We do not doubt the good intentions behind these uses, but we believe that many of them are unhelpful, and some are damaging to Christians seeking to understand God's call. We have also found that some, though not many, emphasize calling as it relates to the Christian's relationship to Christ and the subsequent implications of that relationship as we engage the varied contexts and circumstances of our lives. It is this understanding of calling that we uncover and emphasize in the chapters ahead. Rather than anchor our understanding and use of calling terminology in subjective experiences that emphasize an individualized job, task, or role, we must base our understanding and use of calling in a proper interpretation of the biblical text. A faithful understanding of calling cannot be divorced from the varied experiences that people do have, but it must be congruent with the biblical record and a theological explanation. This will invariably lead us to see calling in terms of our identity in Christ rather than an individualized job, task, passion, or role.

Before we get to our biblical study of calling in chapter 3, we will turn our attention to a broader historical survey of calling. As we survey two thousand years of church history, we will consider how the use of calling terminology has evolved over the centuries. The recent writers we have surveyed in this chapter did not simply invent their understanding of calling and the language used to describe it. Various developments over the course of the centuries have shaped this usage and influenced how many Christians perceive what it means to live faithfully as God's people.

Having a better grasp of the evolution of the church's interpretation of calling over the centuries will help us discern what is worth holding on to, what needs adjusting, and what needs to be let go. With that goal, let us now turn our attention to church history.

2

Looking in the Rearview Mirror

Calling and Vocation throughout Church History

A fish doesn't know it is wet; neither does an Oregonian. This has become the reductionistic and colloquial way in which I (Dan) describe my increasing love for Colorado and my diminishing desire to return to the state in which I was born and raised. In August 2013, our family moved from Salem, Oregon, to Littleton, Colorado, so that I could attend seminary. As the fall months bled into winter, I grew aware that the hems of my pant legs were not perpetually wet, my car did not constantly smell faintly of mildew, and I usually saw a bright orb in the sky during the day. After living in Colorado for nearly a year, I had trouble remembering even five "Oregon-like days," those marked by daylong expressions of gravity-burdened moisture. It was not so much that I hated the rainy environment I grew up in as that I discovered that I loved seeing the sun every day. Moving to Colorado, though, became about much more than mere geographic and meteorological adjustments. I was flourishing in the whole of my life in ways I had never known possible. People still often ask, "Do you think you will ever go back to Oregon?" My quick and clever response: "A fish doesn't know it is wet; neither does an Oregonian."

Sometimes we need to get out of a particular environment in order to understand it with greater objectivity. As we saw in the previous chapter, there are some dominant ways in which calling terminology is used today. These popular uses of calling language have become a given in our discourse with one another. When we know only one way of thinking and living, it is easy to assume that things are simply the way they are. As was the case for this Oregonian with respect to weather, so too is it the case with our contemporary use of calling terminology. We may realize that what we consider obvious about how and to what God calls people may actually be quite contextualized and not as clear as we think.

But for an important biblical and theological concept such as calling and our pursuit of Christian faithfulness, we need to leave our cultural echo chamber in order to evaluate our assumptions. This does not mean that we should abandon everything we have come to believe about calling. But our previous exploration, in chapter 1, of how calling terminology is popularly used—and especially its accompanying shadow side—demands a second look to gain some insight. Perhaps we need to test common assumptions and imagine a recalibrated way forward. To set the stage for this reassessment, we will look into a historical rearview mirror, so to speak, in order to (1) discover and understand how calling has been depicted in different eras of church history and (2) achieve a clearer picture of how calling terminology has come to be used in the church's current teaching on the topic.

As we review these historical accounts, we will find several voices offering insight and wisdom. These sisters and brothers in the faith confront our assumptions and help us recalibrate our understanding and application of a Christian's calling. William Placher's *Callings: Twenty Centuries of Christian Wisdom on*

Vocation is a helpful starting point for our historical survey. He divides two thousand years of church history into four eras: the early church (100–500), the Middle Ages (500–1500), Reformation and post-Reformation (1500–1800), and the post-Christian world (1800–present). Drawing from writings in each era, Placher provides a sweeping overview of how Christians throughout the centuries understood what it means to participate in a larger story.[1] It is this drive toward faithful living amid challenging times that motivates Placher to look backward in order to faithfully move forward. He writes, "The past does not always have the right answers, but its answers are often at least *different* from those of the present, and the differences cause us to question our own previously unexamined assumptions."[2] Through this testing of our assumptions, we can discern what is worth holding on to, what needs adjustment, and what we should let go.

As we begin our assessment of how Christians understood their calling in the early church and into the medieval era, we must consider a couple of methodological points. First, we cannot limit our investigation to the instances in which calling terminology is explicitly used. Although calling terminology abounds in our contemporary culture, the same is not true for the first fifteen centuries of the church's existence, though it is not entirely absent. Calling and vocation terminology did not become prevalent until around the time of the Reformation. When we survey the early church and medieval eras, therefore, we will look at specific uses of calling terminology, but we will also consider the circumstances that led to the more prolific use of calling and vocation terminology during and after the Reformation.

Second, we must be careful not to read our own culturally shaped understanding of calling back into a previous era of church history. When considering calling, we today tend to emphasize the appointing of individuals to specific jobs, tasks, and roles. Though

---

1. Placher, *Callings*, 11.
2. Placher, *Callings*, 3, emphasis original.

there are such accounts in every era of church history,[3] we cannot limit our understanding to these instances. As we survey the various understandings and applications of Christian calling in each era of church history, we will also consider the contextualized circumstances that shaped the church's view of the topic. We will also highlight particular theologians and explore how they understood Christian calling. We will then provide a summary to help us transition into a biblical study of calling in the next chapter. We will start our survey by considering how Christians in the early church understood their calling.

The Early Church (100–500)

Awaiting execution in AD 203, the North African Christian Perpetua refused to recant her faith in Christ. We find her motivation to stand firm recorded in this way: "While we were still under arrest (she said), my father out of love for me was trying to persuade me and shake my resolution. 'Father,' said I, 'do you see this vase here, for example, or water pot or whatever?' 'Yes, I do,' said he. And I told him, 'Could it be called by any other name than what it is?' And he said, 'No.' 'Well, so too I cannot be called anything other than what I am, a Christian.'"[4]

A few generations earlier, the church leader Ignatius of Antioch, who personally knew some of Jesus's first disciples, wrote, "Just pray that I will have strength both outwardly and inwardly so that I may not just talk about it but want to do it, so that I may not merely be called a Christian but actually prove to be one. For if I prove to be one, I can also be called one, and then I will be faithful when I am no longer visible to the world."[5] The words of both Perpetua and Ignatius of Antioch reflect a strong conviction shared

---

3. See "The Life of St. Francis," in Placher, *Callings*, 143–50.
4. "The Martyrdom of Perpetua and Felicity," trans. Musurillo, 109.
5. Ignatius, *To the Romans* 3.2, trans. Holmes, *Apostolic Fathers*, 229. Ignatius also writes about the Christian's identity in his letter *To the Magnesians* 4 and 10.1.

by those in the church's early years. To be called a Christian was far more than a demographic designation or a reflection of family heritage; it was one's identity. The name represented allegiance to Christ in the whole of one's life, and allegiance to Christ was demonstrated by living a certain sort of life, one characterized by faithfulness and Christian virtue. The account of Perpetua's martyrdom closes with the words "Ah, most valiant and blessed martyrs! Truly are you called and chosen for the glory of Christ Jesus our Lord!"[6] Perpetua's calling was not to martyrdom. It was to Christ and thus to be known as a Christian. Her testimony reflected the love and conviction of the One by whom she was known and for whom she gave her life. For her, calling was about identity in Christ and the conviction to live in a manner worthy of her calling to Christ. One's calling to Christ is the dominant way in which the early church understood the Christian's calling.

Around the time John was writing the book of Revelation, 1 Clement was written by Christians in Rome to the Christians in Corinth. In this letter, the Christian's calling is described in singular terms and is found in Christ: "Do we not have one God and one Christ and one Spirit of grace that was poured out upon us? And is there not one calling in Christ?"[7] The Christian's calling is also associated with the church's election in Christ, "through whom he called us from darkness to light, from ignorance to the knowledge of the glory of his name."[8] The letter closes with a doxology, which reinforces the early church's understanding that the Christian's calling is by God through Christ: "The grace of our Lord Jesus Christ be with you and with all people everywhere who have been called by God through him, through whom be glory, honor, power, majesty, and eternal dominion to God, from everlasting to everlasting. Amen."[9]

6. "The Martyrdom of Perpetua and Felicity," trans. Musurillo, 131.
7. From 1 Clem. 46.6, trans. Holmes, *Apostolic Fathers*, 107.
8. From 1 Clem. 59.2, trans. Holmes, *Apostolic Fathers*, 123.
9. From 1 Clem. 65.2, trans. Holmes, *Apostolic Fathers*, 131.

The document titled 2 Clement, written as a sermon rather than a letter, provides more insight into the early church's understanding of its calling. There is one reference to calling in terms of a place,[10] but the remaining uses of the word maintain an emphasis similar to that seen in 1 Clement. Christians were called before they even existed,[11] which is similar to Paul's statement in Eph. 1:4 about the church being chosen before the creation of the world. Calling is equated with salvation in that Christ "has called us children" and "saved us when we were perishing."[12] This calling to salvation resulted in Christians turning from the world and living in light of their hope beyond this life.[13] Their calling to Christ also provided reason for them to repent of their sins: "Therefore, brothers and sisters, inasmuch as we have received no small opportunity to repent, let us, while we still have time, turn again to God who has called us, while we still have one who accepts us."[14] Both 1 and 2 Clement indicate that the early church understood their calling to be in Christ, related to their salvation, and expressed by living in a manner that was different from the world.

The parables in The Shepherd of Hermas also shed some light on the early church's understanding of calling. We find, "All who are called by the name of the Lord came under the shade of the willow," which is a reference to those who have been saved.[15] Later some apostates, who once had responded to God's call, perished because they refused to repent.[16] Calling is also linked to salvation in depicting God's desire toward the unsaved. We read, "But being patient, the Lord wants those who were called through his Son to be saved."[17] There is also a clear link between the person of

---

10. See 2 Clem. 1.2, trans. Holmes, *Apostolic Fathers*, 139.
11. See 2 Clem. 1.8, trans. Holmes, *Apostolic Fathers*, 139.
12. From 2 Clem. 1.4, trans. Holmes, *Apostolic Fathers*, 139.
13. See 2 Clem. 5.1, trans. Holmes, *Apostolic Fathers*, 143.
14. From 2 Clem. 16.1, trans. Holmes, *Apostolic Fathers*, 159.
15. Herm. Sim. 8.1 (67.1), trans. Holmes, *Apostolic Fathers*, 597.
16. Herm. Sim. 8.6 (72.4), trans. Holmes, *Apostolic Fathers*, 609.
17. Herm. Sim. 8.11 (77.1), trans. Holmes, *Apostolic Fathers*, 617.

Jesus Christ and those who are called: "If, therefore, all creation is sustained by the Son of God, what do you think of those who are called by him and bear the name of the Son of God and walk in his commandments?"[18] A final reference links hearing, believing, and receiving the seal with being "called by the name of the Son of God."[19] Similar to the uses in 1 and 2 Clement, these passages further substantiate the claim that the early church understood their calling with reference to salvation in the Son of God and, therefore, to living lives of obedience to him.

Additional early church writers also discuss calling in similar ways. In *The Five Books against Marcion*, Tertullian argues that "all nations [are] being called to His kingdom, from the fact that God set up that kingdom from the tree (of the cross)."[20] He goes on to say that we are to "look at the entire course of His call up to the present time from its beginning, how it is addressed to the nations (Gentiles) who are in these last days approaching to God the Creator."[21] Calling is not spoken of here as an appointment to a job, task, or role, but rather in terms of salvation offered to all people regardless of ethnicity. Justin Martyr also emphasized this same connection between calling and all nations: "But our Jesus, who has not yet come in glory, has sent into Jerusalem a rod of power, namely the word of calling and repentance [meant] for all nations over which demons held sway."[22] In these two examples, calling is spoken of in terms of the salvation that God extends to all people who will repent.

The early church writers use calling terminology far less frequently than we do in our contemporary Christian discourse. Placher observes that "in the early church 'call' (Gk. *klēsis*) usually meant the call to become a Christian."[23] This observation is clearly

---

18. Herm. Sim. 9.14 (91.5), trans. Holmes, *Apostolic Fathers*, 649.
19. Herm. Sim. 9.17 (94.4), trans. Holmes, *Apostolic Fathers*, 655.
20. Tertullian, *Five Books against Marcion* 3.21, trans. ANF 3:339.
21. Tertullian, *Five Books against Marcion* 3.21, trans. ANF 3:340.
22. Justin Martyr, *Dialogue with Trypho* 83, trans. ANF 1:240.
23. Placher, *Callings*, 23.

confirmed by the writers cited above. As more and more people became followers of Christ, the term "Christian" was coined to identify this growing movement by their allegiance to Christ (Acts 11:26).[24] This allegiance led many, including the above-quoted Perpetua, to give their lives for Jesus, the One to whom they were called. Calling was therefore about being called by God to Christ, thus shaping the early Christian identity around this calling. As we now survey the language of "calling" in the Middle Ages, we will see a distinct shift toward calling as a specific role.

The Middle Ages (500–1500)

We now turn our attention to the roughly one thousand years that separated the early church from the Reformation. The Christians who lived during this period were of course not aware of any sort of transition from one era to the next. These distinct eras are marked by historians, who can look back across large swaths of history and identify major movements, patterns, and transition points.[25] To summarize roughly a millennium of church history into neat and tidy categories is impossible. Events in this medieval era, such as the Great Schism between the Eastern Orthodox Church and the Roman Catholic Church (1054) and the Crusades (1096–1291), have forever shaped the church. It will be difficult to address the topic of Christian calling across such a wide historical expanse without being guilty of over-generalizing to some extent, but there are nevertheless distinct characteristics from this era in church history that are helpful for our study.

Let us first consider how the shape of Christian faithfulness evolved from the early church to the medieval era. In the early centuries of the church, calling was for all Christians, who were

24. Bock, *Acts*, 416.
25. See Lynch and Adamo, *Medieval Church*, 12; Evans, *Medieval Theologians*, xiii. For another take on the broad eras of Christian history, see Tickle, *Great Emergence*.

a distinct minority within the broader culture. Christians in the first few centuries were primarily concerned with two things: (1) whether or not to become and remain a Christian and, (2) if a Christian, how public they should be about their faith.[26] Emperor Constantine's conversion is generally considered one of the most significant catalysts for the church's position in and influence on society.[27] Among all the events and movements of the medieval era, "the massive fact of the Middle Ages is the rise of the church as an institution to a place equal to and sometimes greater than the institution of the state."[28] As the centuries marched forward and the church became more organized and influential in the public spheres of society, how Christians understood their calling took on a particular shape. As Christianity grew in public acceptance and adherence, the primary issues of Christian faithfulness came to revolve around whether or not "to choose a celibate life in service of the church."[29] This distinction reveals a significant shift in the broader cultural acceptance of Christianity, which greatly influenced both what it meant to be a Christian and, at times, what it meant for God to "call" someone to a particular task or role.

In the fourth century, following Constantine's conversion to Christianity, the rise of monasticism signaled one of the major and most influential developments of the medieval era. The former way of Christian living—as a minority and often experiencing persecution—was replaced by public acceptance and expanded influence. This resulted in a flood of new converts to the church and led some of the devout to believe the church had become lax in how Christians expressed their faith.[30] Followers of Christ had always emphasized self-denial for the sake of being obedient to God, but this was eventually taken to a new level: "In the fourth and fifth centuries, the ascetic impulse became stronger

26. Placher, *Callings*, 6.
27. Kreider, *Patient Ferment of the Early Church*, 245.
28. Harper and Metzger, *Exploring Ecclesiology*, 57.
29. Placher, *Callings*, 107; Lynch and Adamo, *Medieval Church*, 20.
30. Gregory the Great, *Book of Pastoral Rule*, 11.

and took a new form. As Christian churches became larger and more structured, some fervent Christians saw them as tepid and too compromising with the world. Some of them, mostly men though there were certainly a fair number of women, abandoned urban life and ordinary careers and sought remote places, where they lived lives of systematic and severe self-denial, coupled with prayer and meditation on the scriptures."[31]

Thus monastic life became a preferred way for some to live as Christians. Those who desired to live apart from the world in a more ascetic way of life developed communities built around common rules of life. Monasticism as a movement took on a variety of shapes throughout this era of church history. Despite these differences, there was generally an emphasis on a type of life completely distinct from the rest of those who lived ordinary lives in society. In essence, a division was created between the religious types and everyone else, between the contemplative life and the active life.

Some people today may look back on the monastic movement with a sense of longing, seeking to retrieve practices such as particular forms of prayer and a life of solitude and meditation. They see the appeal of living a reflective life amid a frenetic culture. But there were realities of the monastic life that stand out for our calling investigation. First, to be considered a calling from God—or a vocation, as it would eventually be designated—the monastic life implied that God was intentionally and specifically drawing and inviting someone into this way of life. Often there was a rigorous period of testing to assure that the novice had a genuine divine call to the monastic life. However, the process was seldom so straightforward. Realistically, "what for a few was a choice made consciously and personally as an adult meant for most monks setting out on a road chosen by and directed by others."[32] This was often the case for children whose parents made

31. Lynch and Adamo, *Medieval Church*, 29.
32. Miccoli, "Monks," 65.

the decision to enter them into a monastery at a young age to pursue the monastic life. Becoming a monk, friar, nun, or priest was typically not a personally discerned and specifically defined invitation from God into a religious form of life, though this may have happened for some. More often it was a decision made on behalf of the individual by someone else. In other words, what would eventually be labeled a vocation or a calling by God often was not.

A second point of interest is the "us-and-them" elitist mentality that developed among some living the monastic life. Those, including Christians, who were outside formal religious work did not think of their lives and work in terms of a calling.[33] Those who lived within the religious life—that is, who were "called"— were set apart from those who experienced the "'weaknesses' and the 'woes' of common mortals."[34] This sort of binary thinking was common during the medieval era, and it established the view that those who had a calling were close to God and could find true salvation, and others were left on the outside. Those living in the monastery had a monopoly of sorts on the spiritual life and supposedly were the only ones who understood how to find meaning and purpose in this world as they awaited the next. In essence, the monastic life was "the only full response to Christ's call and was directed toward the eschatological fulfillment of an otherworldly goal."[35] This particular form of the Christian life produced Christians who were convinced that their way of life was superior to all others: "It was presented as a life and a career apart, beginning with its recruitment, entirely or in great part from the very young, since adult vocations, as we have seen, seem to have been the exception for the greater part of this period. . . . It was almost as if monasticism were a reality that in some way

33. Placher, *Callings*, 112.
34. Miccoli, "Monks," 41.
35. Miccoli, "Monks," 53.

claimed to remain closed, impermeable to the memory and the ordinary experience of common mortals."[36] From the first few centuries, the monastics carried forward an emphasis on self-denial and asceticism. But the way this took shape ultimately diverged from the early church's pursuit of unity through love, patience, and humility for all Christians in the world. By attaching the idea of *vocation* to the religious life, a hierarchy developed in which some were more holy than others simply because of their station in life.

Things get more complicated when we consider that monasticism was not the only way for a Christian to acquire holiness or salvation in the medieval era. In a somewhat counterintuitive way of pursuing Christian faithfulness, becoming a soldier and participating in holy war was believed to pave the way for someone to find salvation and holiness. Previously, Christians were discouraged from becoming soldiers. Violence filled the soldier's life, and they were required to attend sacrificial ceremonies, which were not fitting for those who claimed the name of Christ.[37] Eventually, though, warfare became a means by which Christians could become holy: "The notion of holy war, crusade, entered Christianity in the eleventh century, and was directed against the religion which from its earliest days had spoken of holy war, Islam."[38] This additional means to holiness and salvation was contradictory to Jesus's command to turn the other cheek and Paul's admonition to pursue unity through love. But the ends were thought to justify the means, and as a result, warfare was sanctified.

For this time in church history, King Louis IX (1214–1270) of France provides an interesting case study. Although he led two crusades, he was also known to express the sort of virtue and character prized in the early church. He cared for the poor by feeding

36. Miccoli, "Monks," 60.
37. MacCulloch, *Christianity*, 156.
38. MacCulloch, *Christianity*, 382.

them, giving them money, and washing the feet of lepers.[39] This king pursued peace and justice among his subjects while at the same time leading warfare against those adhering to a religion that was different from his own. In this way, being a faithful Christian meant that one could express Christian faithfulness differently in different contexts—acting violently toward some and washing the feet of others. This form of dualistic thinking partially paved the way for the idea that Christians have multiple callings and reinforced a sacred-secular divide in one's personal life.

Throughout the medieval era, we see the church's understanding evolving regarding what it means to be called as God's people. In the early church, calling was about being called by God to Christ, and therefore to living a life identified by obedience and Christlike character. Calling was not individualistic in the sense that each believer had a distinct calling, but rather was applied broadly to all Christians since they were all members of the corporate body of God's people. In the medieval church, virtue was elevated and pursued. But now, having a calling eventually became more about where one lived (such as a monastery) and to what one dedicated their life (asceticism or fighting a holy war). This led to a spiritual distinction and social hierarchy between those who lived the "religious life," meaning those who had vocations, and all others. As well, particular activities (such as warfare) were also callings that led some to salvation and holiness. These distinctive qualities regarding Christian calling bring us to the doorstep of the Reformation, where we will find a significant increase in the specific use of calling and vocation terminology.

Reformation and Post-Reformation Church (1500–1800)

As Emperor Constantine was a hinge between the early church and the medieval church, so Martin Luther became a hinge between

39. John de Joinville, "Chronicle of the Crusade of St. Louis," in Placher, *Callings*, 141–42.

the medieval church and the Reformation.[40] Luther's life and
ministry helped shape the Western church as we know it today.
More specifically, as related to our understanding of calling and
vocation, Luther is indeed a seminal voice. But to understand
Luther's doctrine of vocation, we must first understand a bit
about the man himself. Luther was born into a peasant family,
and his upbringing significantly influenced how he viewed the
world.[41] In the late fifteenth century in northeastern Germany, it
was common for peasants to be farmers. Luther's father, Hans,
was the son of a peasant, but he moved his family to Mansfeld
and began working as a copper miner less than a year after Luther
was born. He eventually partnered with others to own multiple
mineshafts and copper smelters and ran one of the larger operations in Mansfeld.[42]

Life and work were very hard in the world where Luther was
born. Infant mortality rates were very high, plagues and disease
were common, transportation was limited, and many had to beg
for survival.[43] Luther was fortunate, though, to have a father who
found success in work, which allowed Luther to grow up in a
"family who liked their food, enjoyed the pleasures of life, and did
not have to watch the pennies."[44] Luther's upbringing was unique
also in that his mother would stay home with the servants and
children while his father worked in the mines. In most sixteenth-
century urban households, the husband and wife participated
together in the family business.[45] A business partnership between
the husband and wife was normal and necessary to ensure financial security for the wife in case the husband died. Instead of this

40. We will spend considerable time interacting with this era of church history
because of its direct influence on our contemporary understanding of calling and
vocation.

41. Roper, *Martin Luther*, 3.

42. Kittelson and Wiersma, *Luther the Reformer*, 4; see also Roper, *Martin Luther*, 4–6.

43. Kittelson and Wiersma, *Luther the Reformer*, 6.

44. Roper, *Martin Luther*, 8.

45. Roper, *Martin Luther*, 8.

pattern, Luther witnessed a "separation of spheres much more like that of the nineteenth century bourgeoisie, and very different from what was then the norm in early-modern German towns and farmsteads."[46] This separation of spheres was evident not only within his childhood home; Luther also witnessed this at the societal level, for "Mansfeld nurtured in him a sense of politics that was grounded in authority and class division, and rested on a clear distinction between the counts who ruled from the hill and the 'black miners,' as Luther termed them, who worked below."[47] What Luther witnessed in Mansfeld was indeed a reflection of medieval social theory, whereby "all Western European societies in the Middle Ages presumed a division of labor."[48] These divisions separated the roles people played within the church, politics, and the household.[49]

Luther's relatives on his father's side came from peasantry, but relatives on his mother's side—from Eisenach, a town that "boasted churches, monasteries, and books"[50]—were university educated and went on to be doctors, academics, and lawyers. As Luther developed his personal identity within the academic and religious community, "it was his mother's side of the family, not his father's, that exercised a powerful influence."[51] Although he grew up living a relatively comfortable life within a mining community, Luther seemed to favor his maternal heritage over his paternal.

Along with the social and political climate of his time, Luther was also influenced by the religious culture. Sixteenth-century religious beliefs and practices paralleled the way people viewed living in a difficult world. Kittelson and Wiersma observe, "Just as they struggled to achieve material security in their daily lives, they

46. Roper, *Martin Luther*, 8.
47. Roper, *Martin Luther*, 19–20.
48. Kolb, "Called to Milk Cows," 133.
49. Kolb, "Called to Milk Cows," 133–34.
50. Roper, *Martin Luther*, 25.
51. Roper, *Martin Luther*, 25.

also struggled to gain spiritual security."[52] The religious culture consisted of going on pilgrimages, praying to saints and venerating relics, and knowing death and judgment were inevitable.[53] As a result, human effort was a way of earning salvation and security, and "through the power of the church, God would add his grace and smile."[54] Kolb adds, "Medieval European Christianity had defined what it means to be a faithful Christian largely in terms of human performance of sacred ritual and obedience to the sacred persons of the ecclesiastical hierarchy."[55] The ministerial roles of those working for the church were considered more sacred and of greater spiritual significance than those outside the religious establishment.

Luther saw this distinction up close while living in a monastery. Having completed legal studies in Erfurt, lightning struck near Luther while he was out walking one day, and in response he committed himself to becoming a monk. He joined an Augustinian order and "boasted that if ever a pious monk could have gotten to heaven through his monkery, it would have been he."[56] Upon Luther's ordination, his father, Hans, began questioning his son's supposed "call" to the monastic life: "What if that thunderstorm at Stotternheim and your call to the monastery came from the devil?"[57] As Luther continued at the monastery, he began to question much about the church's doctrine, in particular whether his best efforts were enough to please God. The church's system could bring him only so far, and he came to realize that his own works were simply not enough to please God. If the monastic life itself could not bring about the sort of righteousness that saves, then being a monk was not the only way one could be saved and live

52. Kittelson and Wiersma, *Luther the Reformer*, 9.
53. Kittelson and Wiersma, *Luther the Reformer*, 9. See also Kolb, "God Calling," 5.
54. Kittelson and Wiersma, *Luther the Reformer*, 9.
55. Kolb, "Called to Milk Cows," 134.
56. Marty, *Martin Luther*, 9. See also Luther, *Lectures on Galatians* (1535), 13, on Gal. 5:3.
57. Marty, *Martin Luther*, 11.

faithfully as a Christian. Placher summarizes Luther's argument in this way: "No one should feel compelled to enter a monastery or convent and become some sort of super-Christian in order to contribute to one's salvation through works. Rather, we should stick to where God has put us and serve God there."[58] Luther left the monastic life behind and became a key catalyst for the Reformation. There are many doctrinal components to his legacy, but we will concentrate on his thinking about calling and vocation.

Gustaf Wingren observes that it was only after Luther judged the monastic life to be evil in and of itself that he began using "vocation" (German *Beruf*) with greater frequency.[59] To understand Luther's theology, one must draw from different parts of his overall body of work. Through his writings, we can piece together Luther's doctrine of vocation, three features of which we will briefly discuss. First, his understanding of two kinds of righteousness influenced Luther's doctrine of vocation. Luther distinguished between "alien" righteousness, which is the righteousness a person receives from Jesus Christ, and "proper" righteousness, which is the righteousness a person expresses through their actions in relationship to others.[60] In essence, righteousness is first received from Christ through faith, which then enables a person to perform righteous works for their neighbor through their actions. Luther concluded that the righteousness people sought through the church was indeed not righteousness at all, for the commandments of the church were not founded in Scripture but were of human making.[61]

Second, Luther's understanding of the orders of creation and the two kingdoms influenced his doctrine of vocation. He used the metaphor of God's right and left hands to describe the heavenly and earthly kingdoms; the heavenly kingdom was God's "kingdom

58. Placher, *Callings*, 205.
59. Wingren, *Luther on Vocation*, ix. *Vocatio* is the Latin term for calling; *Beruf* is the German word. See also Weber, *Protestant Ethic*, 204–11.
60. Kolb, "God Calling," 5.
61. Kolb, "God Calling," 5.

of the right hand," and the earthly kingdom was God's "kingdom of the left hand."[62] Martin Heinecken suggests that we view the relationship between these two kingdoms as similar to Luther's distinction between the gospel and the law, for God deals with people by "granting men righteousness in the Gospel and ruling and governing the world through the law, that is, through the orders of creation."[63] In his *Commentary on Galatians*, Luther brings together the ideas of two kinds of righteousness and the two kingdoms: "We set up, as it were, two worlds, one heavenly . . . and one earthly. . . . Each has its own kind of righteousness. The righteousness of the law is earthly, concerned with earthly affairs and consists of our doing of good works. . . . The heavenly, passive righteousness is not of ourselves; we receive it from heaven. We do not produce it but receive it in faith."[64]

Third, Luther's understanding of the term "calling" shaped his doctrine of vocation. Volf observes that "one of Luther's most culturally influential accomplishments was to overcome the monastic reduction of *vocatio* to a calling to a particular kind of religious life."[65] Luther believed that there were two vocations for every Christian: a spiritual and an external. The former referred to God's call to the individual to enter the kingdom of God; the latter is "God's call to serve God and one's fellow human beings in the world."[66] Luther distinguished between these two callings in his commentary on 1 Cor. 7:24 by showing the difference between a person's status in being married or being a priest (external) and the status a person has in being called to Christ (spiritual).[67]

Luther understood external vocation to be the different stations people held in life, based on the social structures that were in place. Kolb comments that according to Luther, "Believers recognize that

---

62. Kolb, "God Calling," 5.
63. Heinecken, "Luther and the 'Orders of Creation,'" 395.
64. Wingren, *Luther on Vocation*, 14–15.
65. Volf, *Work in the Spirit*, 105.
66. Volf, *Work in the Spirit*, 105–6.
67. Luther, *Luther's Works*, 28:46.

God has placed them in the structures of human life created by God and has called them to the tasks of caring for other creatures, human and otherwise, as agents of God's providential presence and care."[68] This calling, which all believers have, could be expressed within the family and economic roles found within medieval households. This meant vocation was not limited to those in "religious" positions, such as monks and priests. Instead, all people had a calling by which they were to serve others. As such, the direction of one's calling was to the particular stations and tasks that were in front of them. This also meant that any type of work could be a vocation.[69] Luther unmasked the cultural ideology of his day, which had determined the sacredness and significance of various kinds of work based on the division of labor that existed within medieval society.[70]

Though he may have been one of the most influential Reformation voices regarding calling and vocation, Luther was not the only one thinking and writing about these matters. From a different geographic and economic situation, John Calvin offered his own insights on the topic. Luther came from rural, feudal Germany and was concerned with tensions between peasants and nobles.[71] His concerns around work and vocation focused on the way in which Christians loved their neighbors through their assigned stations in life rather than on the economic possibilities and realities of growing urban contexts. Calvin, on the other hand, lived in Geneva, which operated with a developing capitalist economy. As a result, he was aware of the economic possibilities and the ways in which people in general worked and especially of how Christians could express their faith in and through their work. Both Luther and Calvin concurred that the Christian must serve God in the world. Luther argued that one should be content

---

68. Kolb, "Called to Milk Cows," 135.

69. Volf, *Work in the Spirit*, 105.

70. We draw the concept of unmasking cultural ideologies from Newbigin, *Truth to Tell*, 77.

71. McGrath, *Life of John Calvin*, 230.

to remain in the station in life to which God had called them. Calvin partially agreed yet "allowed for some social motion from one job to another and thought that some government officials had a calling to stand up for the rights of the people against the wishes of tyrants."[72]

For Calvin, a Christian could experience two different callings: "There is the universal call which consists in the outward preaching of the gospel, by which the Lord invites all men without distinction to come to him. . . . There is another—special—call, in which practically none but believers are made to share when, through the inward illumination of his Spirit, God causes his teaching to take root in their hearts."[73] In the midst of life's circumstances, the Christian is supposed to look to this calling amid their "appointed duties. . . . Therefore each individual has his own kind of living assigned to him by the Lord as a sort of sentry post so that he may not heedlessly wander throughout life."[74] These appointed duties supply a third type of calling a Christian could experience. Similar to Luther's belief that God calls Christians to particular stations in life, Calvin utilizes the phrase "modes of living": "God distinguishes between our various situations and our modes of living, and lays down the tasks each of us is to fulfil. And so that no one should lightly go beyond his limits, he has termed such modes of living 'callings.' Thus we should all regard our particular situation as a post assigned to us by God, lest in the course of our lives we flit to and fro and drift aimlessly about."[75]

Like Luther, Calvin also referenced 1 Cor. 7 regarding how Christians should understand their public expression of God's calling to specific stations and modes of living. "Mundane labour became an integral part of Calvin's spirituality, lending a

72. Placher, *Callings*, 207.
73. Calvin, *Institutes of the Christian Religion*, 490.
74. Calvin, *Calvin's Institutes*, 92.
75. Calvin, *Institutes of the Christian Religion*, 821.

new meaning to the medieval monastic slogan *laborare est orare*, 'to labour is to pray.' Manual labour was not simply the norm at Geneva; it was the religiously sanctioned ideal. For the first time, the ordinary everyday activity of even the most petty producer was given a religious significance. Action in the world was dignified and sanctified."[76]

Luther and Calvin are recognized as theological giants of the Reformation, but they were not the only Reformation-era voices offering insights into calling and vocation. William Perkins taught at Cambridge in the sixteenth century and defined vocation or calling as "a certain kind of life, ordained and imposed on man by God for the common good."[77] He emphasized a Christian's two callings: the first being the general calling to Christ, and the second being quite particular and personal: "the execution of some particular office, arising of that distinction which God makes between man and man in every society."[78] This particular calling was reserved for specific people in specific roles: magistrate, minister, and master.[79] While Perkins seems to limit particular callings to those in specific societal roles, he also claims, "Every person, of every degree, sex, or condition without exception must have some personal and particular calling to walk in."[80] Regardless of one's particular calling, it "must be practiced in and with the general calling of a Christian" and be rendered as service to God and others.[81]

Richard Baxter was a church leader, hymn writer, and theologian who lived in England in the seventeenth century. He defined a calling as "a stated, ordinary course of labor."[82] Ideally,

76. McGrath, *Life of John Calvin*, 233.
77. Perkins, "Treatise of the Vocations," 262. See also Winstanley's "Declaration from the Poor" as an example of someone else who emphasized the notion of the Christian's responsibility toward pursuing the common good in society.
78. Perkins, "Treatise of the Vocations," 265.
79. Perkins, "Treatise of the Vocations," 265.
80. Perkins, "Treatise of the Vocations," 266.
81. Perkins, "Treatise of the Vocations," 269.
82. Baxter, "Directions about Our Labor and Callings," 281.

all people had some sort of job, which equated to their calling.
He also emphasized pursuing the public good but advocated for
a hierarchy of callings within society: "The callings most useful
to the public good are the magistrates, the pastors, and teachers of the church, schoolmasters, physicians, lawyers, husband-
men (ploughmen, graziers, and shepherds); and next to them are
mariners, clothiers, booksellers, tailors, and such others that are
employed about things most necessary to mankind."[83] If someone had the opportunity to choose a particular type of calling,
and two callings appeared to have the same sort of public benefit
to others, Baxter instructed them to choose the calling that was
more advantageous to their soul as opposed to being advantageous
regarding monetary gain.[84]

William Law, a Church of England priest, lived during the eigh-
teenth century. Rather than emphasizing specific types of work
as callings, he focused on holy living in the whole of one's life.
When he refers to a person's multiple callings, functionally he
is referring to the various contexts of one's life. Unlike Baxter,
Law did not focus on a value hierarchy between different types of
work. He did, however, distinguish between the work of clergy and
the work all other kinds of workers perform. Clergy "must live
wholly unto God in one particular way, that is, in the exercise of
holy offices, in the ministration of prayers and sacraments, and a
zealous distribution of spiritual goods."[85] Those in other types of
employments were "as much obliged to act as the servants of God,
and live wholly unto Him in their several callings."[86] Within all
types of work, Law valued the manner in which someone engages
the work more than the nature of the work itself. He believed
that one should not pursue wealth and riches at the expense of
demonstrating honesty, fairness, justice, and selflessness.

83. Baxter, "Directions about Our Labor and Callings," 283.
84. Baxter, "Directions about Our Labor and Callings," 283.
85. Law, "Serious Call to a Devout and Holy Life," 305.
86. Law, "Serious Call to a Devout and Holy Life," 305.

The Reformation did indeed bring about reform in Christians' understanding and application of calling and vocation. The Reformers and post-Reformers expanded calling and vocation to apply to all types of work and all stations of life. Religious work was not excluded from the sort of work one could do as a calling, but neither did it monopolize what constituted a calling. This provides the major backdrop to the twentieth century, where a particular view of calling and vocation cemented itself in the minds and lives of Christians throughout the Western world: calling describes what a person is particularly fashioned to accomplish in the world, and more specifically, how God has wired a person to fulfill that task or function. As we will see, this popular understanding of calling and vocation continued evolving, especially throughout the twentieth century. Some Christians continued reinforcing this work-calling focus, but others recognized the shortcomings of this emphasis. As we will see in the next section, the contextualized circumstances of a person's life play a critical role in shaping their understanding and application of calling and vocation and the assumptions that they test.

Post-Christian Church (1800–Present)

Although Constantine and Luther served as key transition figures between the early church and the medieval-era church and between the Middle Ages and the Reformation, respectively, the transition to the post-Christian church does not have a similar transition figure. Instead, as we move through this historical period, we will consider key thinkers who specifically reflected on calling and vocation within their own contexts.[87] The nineteenth century saw a continued emphasis on God's specific appointment to particular work. John Henry Newman and Horace Bushnell are

---

87. There is no way to include every person who wrote about calling and vocation in this era of church history. We have chosen individuals who provide unique perspectives that do not necessarily reinforce the commonly held view of calling-as-work.

two examples of those who continued to reinforce a view of calling that emphasized God's sovereign appointment to particular jobs and work.[88] Moving into the twentieth century, equating calling and vocation with work remained the norm, but the view was shaped in various ways as different thinkers considered, in light of their particular circumstances, what it means to be called. As we bring our survey to the present, the following limited snapshots represent the nuanced ways in which Christians promoted calling and vocation.

Max Weber (1864–1920)

Max Weber, a German sociologist and philosopher in the latter part of the nineteenth century and into the first part of the twentieth century, wrote *The Protestant Ethic and the Spirit of Capitalism*, which some consider "one of the most important works of sociology and economics ever written."[89] One of Weber's key contributions is his observation that capitalism is the chosen economic system within predominantly Protestant countries and the reason for the economic success of those countries. It is not simply that a country is Protestant, though, that leads toward economic success. Rather, Weber ties economic success to the significance and meaning people find in their work, which derives from a personal sense of calling attached to making money through one's work. Weber observes, "The capitalistic system so needs this devotion to the calling of making money, it is an attitude toward material goods which is so well suited to that system, so intimately bound up with the conditions of survival in the economic struggle for existence."[90] Ultimately, certain religious ideas developed a particular economic ethos that prevailed within Western capitalistic countries.[91]

---

88. See Placher, *Callings*, 343–49, 353–59.
89. Barnes, *Redeeming Capitalism*, 59.
90. Weber, *Protestant Ethic*, 72; on p. 77, Weber also claims that a person's calling to a task "is necessary to capitalism."
91. Weber, *Protestant Ethic*, 27.

At the time of Weber's writing, vocation was functionally defined as "a life task, a definite field in which to work."[92] This is in keeping with developments within and after the Reformation. Although he draws from Luther's belief that a person is called to a particular station in life in order to serve their neighbor, Weber goes further and recognizes the importance of a person finding meaning and significance in their calling, or the tasks of their work. This sort of significance becomes a powerful force that compels someone to view their work as ordained by God.

Dietrich Bonhoeffer (1906–1945)

Bonhoeffer was a German pastor and theologian during the first half of the twentieth century. Popularly known for his participation in an unsuccessful attempt to kill Hitler, which ultimately cost him his life, Bonhoeffer left behind a valuable corpus of writing that is quite relevant for our own cultural moment. Some consider *Ethics* to be his magnum opus, which he wrote as a personal defense, of sorts, for his decision to participate in an attempt on Hitler's life. It also cast a vision for a new way for Christians to live in the world after World War II. Bonhoeffer dedicated a portion of *Ethics* to reflecting particularly on calling and vocation.

Bonhoeffer's statements in *Ethics* describe vocation as "the place of responsibility."[93] His understanding of calling is anchored in Christ: "In encounter with Jesus Christ, a person experiences God's call [*Ruf*], and in it the calling [*Berufung*] to a life in community with Jesus Christ. . . . From Christ's perspective this life is now my vocation; from my own perspective it is my responsibility."[94]

92. Weber, *Protestant Ethic*, 79. Weber acknowledges the language evolution that took place over centuries as Hebrew, Greek, Latin, and German terms were used at various times to communicate this idea of God's calling; see his endnotes 1, 2, and 3 on 204–10 for an extensive linguistic study.
93. Bonhoeffer, *Ethics*, 289.
94. Bonhoeffer, *Ethics*, 290.

This responsibility follows Luther's emphasis to serve and love one's neighbor, but service to one's neighbor is not limited to one's gainful employment. For Bonhoeffer, calling is not about a definite field of activity or reduced to one's occupation but rather extends to the whole of one's life. He writes, "Vocation is responsibility, and responsibility is the whole response of the whole person to reality as a whole. This is precisely why a myopic self-limitation to one's vocational obligations in the narrowest sense is out of the question; such a limitation would be irresponsibility."[95] Our generation today is not the first to myopically apply calling to a particular dimension of one's life, often to one's occupational work. Bonhoeffer reveals an important inconsistency regarding faithful Christian responsibility when one limits the scope of one's calling.

Bonhoeffer's particular reflections about calling and vocation include significant, concrete applications in the real world. By way of illustration, Bonhoeffer cites the Scottsboro, Alabama, case of 1931:

> In a terrible miscarriage of justice in the United States in 1931, nine young black men accused of raping a white girl of dubious reputation were sentenced to death even though their guilt could not be proven. This triggered a storm of outrage that found expression in open letters from the most respected European public figures. A Christian, disturbed by these events, asked a leading church official in Germany to consider raising his voice also in protest against the case. For his refusal to do so, the official cited the "Lutheran" understanding of vocation, that is, the limitation of the extent of his responsibility. But in fact it was the protest from all around the world that eventually led to the revision of the verdict.[96]

95. Bonhoeffer, *Ethics*, 293.
96. Bonhoeffer, *Ethics*, 295. See also Williams, *Bonhoeffer's Black Jesus*, 22–23. While Bonhoeffer references the Scottsboro case in the third person in *Ethics*, Williams argues that this was indeed Bonhoeffer's personal account as the one entreating the leading church official in Germany.

Even as a Lutheran pastor, Bonhoeffer recognized both the limitations and the shortcomings of Luther's doctrine of vocation. Rather than truncate his understanding and application of Christian responsibility, though, Bonhoeffer ultimately understood calling in terms of a scope of responsibility, and in particular, a scope that extends to the whole of one's life. Christians are not responsible to meet all the needs of the world, but if a particular opportunity arises for them to responsibly engage the needs of the world, they are to faithfully do so because of who they are in Christ.

Karl Barth (1886–1968)

Karl Barth, considered by many to be one of the most influential theologians of the twentieth century, was a contemporary of Bonhoeffer and agreed with him that vocation and calling are not limited to one's work. He observes, "That a man's vocation is exhausted in his profession is no more true than that God's calling which comes to him is simply an impulsion to work. He will always live in widely different spheres if he receives the divine calling and is obedient to it."[97] Barth also writes extensively about Christian vocation as it relates to living in light of the reality of Christ. In his *Church Dogmatics*, Barth discusses how the event of vocation and the goal of vocation are living in union with Christ.[98] Rhys Kuzmič provides helpful insight regarding Barth's use of *Beruf* (vocation) and *Berufung* (calling). He observes that *Beruf* is about a person's action in a particular context within the world, and *Berufung* is about one's calling in Christ: "Vocation (*Beruf*) for Barth is the totality of the individual's socio-historical context which that individual brings to the hearing of the divine call (*Berufung*)."[99]

Barth was critical of Luther's interpretation of 1 Cor. 7:20. He did not want to conflate the call from above with a particular

97. Barth, *Church Dogmatics*, III/4:265.
98. Barth, *Church Dogmatics*, IV/3.2:123–81.
99. Kuzmič, "*Beruf* and *Berufung*," 265.

station in life as Luther did.[100] While Bonhoeffer emphasized the scope of one's responsibility, Barth emphasized the particularities of one's life and the freedom we have within these particularities to act in obedience to the calling we have to Christ: "In its reality vocation is the whole of the particularity, limitation, and restriction in which every man meets the divine call and command, which wholly claims him in the totality of his previous existence, and to which above all wholeness and therefore total differentiation and specification are intrinsically proper as God intends and addresses this man and not another."[101] As believers discern how to live obediently to Christ based upon their specific context, they are to do so within the reality of their limitations. Just as an artist is limited by the medium within which they choose to create, so too is the Christian bound by the limitations of their circumstances. Within these limitations, though, there is freedom to operate and live faithfully.[102] Thus Barth argues that there is a distinct and particular shape to our obedience in response to our calling in Christ. As life's circumstances change, so too does the shape of one's obedience. But the Christian's calling to Christ does not ultimately change.

Dorothy Sayers (1893–1957)

Sayers was a writer and a medieval literature scholar at Oxford. Though not a professional theologian or biblical scholar, she reflected on the purpose and place of work as a Christian, doing so in the midst of World War II, and offers a useful insight for us. At that time, women were asked to leave their homes and engage in "the men's work" because of the labor shortage created by the war.[103] When the men returned from the war, women returned to their work within their homes. Sayers sees calling,

---

100. Kuzmič, "*Beruf* and *Berufung*," 265–66.
101. Barth, *Church Dogmatics*, III/4:265.
102. We will further discuss Barth's understanding of limitations in chap. 5.
103. Sayers, "Vocation in Work," 410.

vocation, and work as intertwined in a manner similar to the views of Bonhoeffer and Barth. Work is *related* to calling and vocation, but the extent of one's vocation cannot be *limited* to one's employment. Sayers was not content to use the unique circumstances of a wartime economy as an excuse to exploit workers, some of whom had ordinary but necessary jobs, such as the factory hand who "endlessly and monotonously [pushes] a pin into a slot."[104]

Sayers sees God as a Maker, who made people in his image to be makers themselves: "Man is a maker, who makes things because he wants to, because he cannot fulfill his true nature if he is prevented from making things for the love of the job. He is made in the image of the Maker, and he must himself create or become something less than man."[105] As such, there is a clear emphasis on the relationship between people and God in their work because he has made them to work.[106] Using the example of an artist, Sayers argues that there needs to be something more to a person's vocation than merely being employed. Meaning and satisfaction in work are more closely related to vocation than simply being employed and earning a wage. Sayers argues against equating calling with employment, saying, "We can measure the distance we have fallen from the idea that work is a vocation to which we are called, by the extent to which we have come to substitute the word 'employment' for 'work.'"[107] In doing so, Sayers looked toward theology rather than economics for her understanding of calling and vocation. As a result, calling and vocation cannot and should not be understood in terms of what one does for gainful employment. Calling and vocation, rooted in who we are as created in God's image, should impact what a person does for pay but should never be equated with it.

104. Sayers, "Vocation in Work," 411.
105. Sayers, "Vocation in Work," 406.
106. Sayers, *Letters to a Diminished Church*, 117.
107. Sayers, "Vocation in Work," 409.

Conclusion

History is a record of reactions and counterreactions to certain movements and ideas. We often describe these alternations as pendulum swings. A simple example is how children grow up determined to parent their kids differently than the way they themselves were parented. While there is likely continuity between one's parents and one's own beliefs and behaviors, there are often ways in which a child swings the pendulum, so to speak, and intentionally does something different from their parents as a counterreaction. Throughout two thousand years of church history, we see the same dynamic at work in how Christians have understood and applied God's calling.

In the early church, to be called was to be a Christian and to behave like a Christian. As the medieval era unfolded, the formal ecclesial roles within the church monopolized the calling conversation. To be called was primarily to be a priest, monk, nun, or perhaps a soldier in conquest of the holy land. Martin Luther, John Calvin, and other Reformers pushed back against this emphasis on religious roles and lifted up all types of work as callings. This same conflation of calling and work continued through the Puritan era. While some, like Barth and Bonhoeffer, presented a more holistic view of calling, their perspectives are in the minority, and people's occupations continued to garner the most attention in relation to calling and vocation. In the twentieth century, with the increase of occupational ministry roles such as pastors and missionaries and the reality that one could earn a living through the ministry profession, the pendulum swung back toward religious work as callings. As seen in the previous chapter, the work of pastors and missionaries especially came to monopolize the calling conversation.

The current iteration of the Faith at Work Movement is tackling this pendulum swing head-on as Luther did. Most of those writing about calling do not deny that God appoints some to particular professional ministry roles, but pastors, theologians, and writers such as Tim Keller, Tom Nelson, Amy Sherman, and R. Paul Ste-vens endorse a view of calling that extends to all kinds of work.[108] The tendency to conflate calling and work is understandable, but we hope to demonstrate that although calling includes one's work (for that is indeed a significant context for many people), it must extend further to encompass the whole of one's life. Today's popu-lar discourse on callings typically revolves around middle-upper class, white-collar work. While there has been an increased interest in addressing blue-collar workers,[109] we must be careful to avoid unintentionally patronizing those working in these jobs or living below the poverty line.

What are we to make of how views on calling and vocation have evolved over the centuries and, in particular, the variety of ways in which the words "calling" and "vocation" are used today? Before we answer this question, we should consider how calling terminology is used in the Bible. After all, how the Scriptures define calling should dominate our understanding. In fact, we believe it could revolutionize our thinking!

108. See chap. 1 above on how these examples reinforce the popularly held view that a person's work in the world is at least part of their calling.
109. See Haanen, "God of the Second Shift."

3

Calling in the Bible

In chapters 1 and 2 we described the confusing historical setting for our study. Where do we go next? As Christians concerned to understand this very crucial topic, it is natural but also vital that we hear what the Bible has to say about it. We have already seen that writers, speakers, and various other sources throughout history use "call," "calling," and "vocation" in a bewildering variety of ways. In Lewis Carroll's *Through the Looking Glass*, Humpty Dumpty was correct in insisting that he can make a word mean anything he wants, but we believe that some words should be used precisely as the writers of Scripture intend them to be understood. We contend that there is much to gain from using terms in a manner consistent with their biblical use, and the meaning of "call" is very robust and important. As we have already seen, by misusing this rich term, we are left with anemic and confusing understandings. We must go back to the Scriptures.

As we begin our survey and analysis of key verses, we need to establish two fundamental points of biblical interpretation. They may strike you as obvious, but these principles are violated or misunderstood so frequently that it is crucial to clarify this at the outset. First, we believe that the goal of interpretation is to discover the meaning the biblical authors intended at the time of writing. We should not impose a later or ill-fitting meaning that the original authors and readers would not have intended or understood.[1] What did the authors intend to communicate to their readers? This is crucial, for we believe the Holy Spirit spoke God's intended message through human authors.

Second, we must distinguish between what is *descriptive* in Scripture and what is presented as *prescriptive* or *normative*. This distinction is especially crucial when reading narrative texts, but it also applies to other types of biblical literature. To what extent is what we read normative for God's people? In the case of a narrative text, the author describes the words and actions of the biblical characters, but readers must determine whether what happened is normative. That is, does the description of the incident prescribe what we should do or what will happen? Or put differently, is there a normative principle growing out of the biblical usage that we ought to apply today?

The biblical authors may describe or present incidents or teachings in the Bible that they (and thus the Holy Spirit) intend as normative teaching for God's people. For example, the account of Cain's murder of his brother Abel (or Moses of the Egyptian, or David of Uriah) is expressed in negative terms, but this does not merely describe an unfortunate incident. We are to learn a normative principle: murder violates God's will. The sixth commandment confirms this judgment.

On the other hand, some incidents or teachings may merely describe what happened in a specific situation with no intention of setting a precedent for the future. Let's illustrate this with both an incident and a teaching.

Luke reports a disturbing incident involving Ananias and Sapphira in Acts 5:1–11.[2] The author *describes* what happened be-

---

1. On the goal of interpretation, see W. Klein, Blomberg, and Hubbard, *Introduction to Biblical Interpretation*, 244–92.
2. We will assume the traditional Lukan authorship of Acts. Nothing in our study hinges on whether that attribution is correct or not. We take the same approach with other NT books and authors.

cause of this couple's lying to the church (and to God): they were struck dead. But the divine judgment of killing is not *normative*. That is, this incident does not *prescribe* a divine action; God does not always strike liars dead in the church.[3] We well learn how much God detests such hypocrisy (other biblical texts or incidents may confirm this principle as normative), but the specific action God took back then is not normative. Luke reports that because of a vow he had taken, Paul got a haircut when he stopped in Cenchreae (Acts 18:18). However, it is not normative for a Christian who takes a vow to get a haircut,[4] much less to go to Cenchreae for it!

Biblical writers sometimes give instruction or a ruling based on a particular situation arising in their cultural context. In 1 Cor. 11:5, for example, Paul instructs the Christian women in Corinth to have their heads covered in worship (whether the intended covering was a veil or long hair need not detain us here).[5] Surely Paul assumes a principle behind this instruction, but most readers recognize that covering the head is not a normative practice for all Christian women to follow when in church.[6] In 1 Cor. 11, Paul *describes* a situation and gives his instruction to correct some serious infractions in the Corinthians' church practices. Though we can learn principles from Paul's instructions and why he gave them, the ruling itself was for a particular time and cultural context, and the practice of covering the head in worship is not normative for all women and all churches thereafter.

As we seek to interpret the biblical authors' teaching about what is normative for our understanding of God's call, we will find some

---

3. At the same time, we can never say God won't or can't inflict physical punishments on those who violate his will. Paul hints at this in 1 Cor. 11:30 while addressing the Corinthians' abuse of the Lord's Supper.

4. Christians may of course choose of their own accord to implement the principle here of engaging in a concrete action to cement some vow or promise made to God.

5. For helpful discussions of the alternatives, see Fee, *First Epistle to the Corinthians*, 560–68; Ciampa and Rosner, *First Letter to the Corinthians*, 511–23.

6. We acknowledge that some church traditions do believe women should wear head coverings as a normative practice.

striking examples of what is often termed a "call" from God. Yet we always need to raise the question of normativity. Neither how God called Isaiah (see Isa. 6 for the description; cf. 49:1) nor how he called Jeremiah (Jer. 1:4–10) necessarily prescribes how God calls people to serve him today. So, what is the normative understanding of God's call? We believe that we can answer that, and to do so, we need to survey the biblical evidence.

How is "calling" used in the Bible? The answer will require that we study key terms such as "call" and "calling," of course,[7] but we often find the semantic idea of a divine call or calling in other terms and passages that do not employ explicit calling language. Our investigation must include terms or concepts such as "God's will," "appointment," "choose," and "elect" in order to gain a clearer picture of what God's call on a person's life entails.

Calling in the Old Testament

As soon as we consider what "calling" means in the OT, we discover a phenomenon that extends throughout the Bible and has profound implications for our understanding. What do we mean? We must recognize both an individual and a corporate use of our terms. That is, God calls individuals, but he also calls corporate bodies such as Israel and the church. We will first survey the call of individuals, which is expressed predominantly in the language of *election*: God chose or appointed individuals to serve him. Is this equivalent to saying that they have a call from God?

Call of Individuals

We will look at some representative individuals whom God chose to serve him. Many consider Gen. 12:1–5 to be the "call of Abram," but no explicit calling language occurs in this section. The NT writer of Hebrews does, however, use the Greek verb for

---

7. We will conduct our word studies on the relevant Hebrew or Greek terms.

"call" when referring to this incident (Heb. 11:8).[8] The Genesis account begins simply with "And the LORD said to Abram, 'Go,'" and God promises that greatness and blessing (Gen. 12:1–3) will follow Abram's response: "So Abram went as the LORD had told him" (12:4). Later, the writer of Nehemiah says that "the LORD God . . . *chose* Abram" (Neh. 9:7, emphasis added). We soon notice that what people often see as God's "call" overlaps with the biblical language of "choose/elect."

We find God's "call" of Moses in Exod. 3:1–15 (cf. 4:10–17). After getting Moses's attention through the burning bush, God *calls* (Hb. *qārā'*; Gk. *kaleō* in the LXX) Moses to listen to him (3:4). What God tells Moses amounts to a divine commission: "So now, go. I am sending you to Pharaoh to bring my people the Israelites out of Egypt" (Exod. 3:10). In Num. 16:5, 7 the verb "choose" is used to refer to God's appointment of Moses, and in Ps. 106:23 Moses is called God's chosen one. As for Joshua, after serving as Moses's aide (Exod. 33:11; Num. 11:28; Deut. 1:38), God commissions him to be Moses's successor (Deut. 31:14, 23). Then by the laying on of hands, Moses makes the succession plan official (Deut. 34:9). The book of Joshua begins with God's instructions to Joshua to take the land that God is giving to the Israelites (Josh. 1:1–9). No specific "calling" or election language appears in these reports concerning Joshua.

While David was still a shepherd boy, the prophet Samuel anointed him as the future king of Israel (1 Sam. 16:1–13). King Saul learns that God has removed him from the throne and "appointed" David in his place (1 Sam. 13:13–14; cf. 2 Sam. 6:21; Ps. 78:70). No specific calling language occurs.

---

8. The common Hebrew verb for "call" is *qārā'* (קָרָא), occurring about 880 times in the OT. *HALOT* (1128–31) gives its meanings: "call, give a name to, invoke, summon, summon an assembly, proclaim, call on, appeal to, invite, recite from." Many of these overlap with the Greek words for "call," *kaleō* (καλέω) and its cognates. For more on *qārā'* see *NIDOTTE* 3:971–74; *TDOT* 13:109–35. For a full discussion of election language in the OT, see W. Klein, *New Chosen People*, 3–18. For the uses of *kaleō* in the LXX, see *NIDNTTE* 2:602–4.

What about Israel's prophets? In a spectacular and familiar scene, God issues his invitation to Isaiah to prophesy to Israel (Isa. 6:1–8). Later Isaiah asserts that God called him before his birth (49:1). God appoints Jeremiah to be a prophet (Jer. 1:4–8). Ezekiel's appointment to become a prophet is quite dramatic (Ezek. 2:1–3). Jonah provides an example of a prophet who, at least initially, rejects God's call: "The word of the LORD came to Jonah son of Amittai: 'Go to the great city of Nineveh and preach against it, because its wickedness has come up before me'" (Jon. 1:1–2). Amos explains his position this way: "The LORD took me from tending the flock and said to me, 'Go, prophesy to my people Israel'" (Amos 7:15). In these prophetic appointments, apart from one reference in Isa. 49:1, we find no language of calling, only commands to go and prophesy.

Corporate Calling

Priests and Levites possess a "call" to serve in their various capacities. But we consider this a corporate calling (or election) since individual priests occupy their positions as part of a hereditary appointment (see 1 Chron. 15:2; 2 Chron. 29:11; Deut. 18:5; 21:5). God disqualifies individual priests when they prove unsuitable (e.g., Korah, Num. 16; Eli's sons, 1 Sam. 2). And though we have cited Saul and David as individuals appointed by God, we might also view the monarchy as a corporate "calling." The individual kings' calling and mission are bound up with God's election of the nation to be God's people (Pss. 28:8; 72:1–2), and they are warned in Deuteronomy to appoint as kings only those whom "the LORD . . . chooses" (Deut. 17:15).

The dominant instance of a corporate call is God's choice of the nation Israel to be his treasured people.[9] The writers make clear that being or identity is the key to Israel's election. Israel is chosen to *be* God's holy people and treasured possession, but this

9. Among the key texts, see Deut. 7:6; 10:15; 14:2; Isa. 41:8–9; and Ps. 132:13–14.

call comes with responsibilities. God chooses Israel to *be* a righteous people, a nation that fulfills God's will and displays godly virtues like obedience, justice, and compassion (see Deut. 7:6–12, 19–20; 10:15–22). Obedience brings blessing. The nation's failure to embrace its calling incurs God's judgment (Deut. 4:39–40; Ezek. 16:4–14, 35–58).

The OT writers are clear about the purpose of Israel's election. Isaiah proclaims: "Listen to me, my people; hear me, my nation: Instruction will go out from me; my justice will become a light to the nations" (51:4); "Nations will come to your light, and kings to the brightness of your dawn" (60:3). God's call of Israel is due to God's sovereign choice, not to any inherent virtue or value in Israel. The point of the call is service, and this obligation continues throughout Israel's history (Amos 3:2; 9:7). Each generation needs to affirm God's covenant for itself, and each individual Israelite is required to keep the terms or risk being cut off from the people (see Exod. 12:19; Num. 19:13). The writers seem to distinguish between God's call or choice of the corporate nation as God's chosen people, and the fate of individual Jews who may or may not remain within that people to enjoy the benefits of God's call. Indeed, despite Israel's repeated unfaithfulness, resulting in divine chastening (Amos 3:2), God proves faithful to his people, and Israel survives (Ezek. 16:59–60).

Conclusions about Calling in the Old Testament

The concept of choice or election seems to be the most revealing terminology the OT writers use to describe the action of God in summoning, appointing, or calling someone to serve him—whether that be individuals, the priesthood, or the nation Israel. Clearly, key figures in the history and life of Israel (e.g., Abram, Moses, the priests, kings, and prophets) were appointed to their tasks or roles by God's choice. In that sense we might say they were "called" to their roles, though it is more precise to say that God chose or appointed them. We must underscore the exceptional nature of this nomenclature. Appointment or election language applies to central figures in Israel, not common people. Individual Israelites have no "calling" other than to *be* faithful members of the elect, covenant community, though that obligation is very important. That is, their "calling" as God's people requires obedience and holiness since they have that identity, a nation chosen to be a witness to the surrounding nations. Their calling is corporate as members of the people of God.

What about *descriptive* versus *normative*? On an individual level we encounter God's choice of key persons in Israel. Their disparate circumstances prior to God's choice make it difficult to discern any clear patterns for normativity. Whether Abram, Moses, or the prophets, God sovereignly chooses them. The texts give us no clues about whether they have any sense of "calling" or aspire to a "vocation" as the terms are often employed today. Nor do the OT writers encourage the original readers of these texts (or subsequent ones) to ask whether God is "calling" them to serve as prophets or in other leadership roles.[10] God inaugurates the monarchy; after a disastrous selection of Saul, God establishes the Davidic dynasty. The sons of Aaron are priests. The prophets are often inadvertent or surprised candidates for their roles. Again, no texts seem to support the idea of individuals seeking some special call or possessing some mystical sense of God's call.

On the other hand, the normative element of God's "call" on the people of Israel (both corporate and individual) is to serve God in holiness and obedience—to fulfill the terms of the covenant that God has determined for his people. This is no esoteric call; nor does it require special discernment. These covenantal terms are specified in many texts within the pages of Holy Scripture.

---

10. We recognize that NT writers speak of the spiritual gift of "prophecy." As with other gifts that the Spirit gives to the church, believers are encouraged to discover and use their gifts for the benefit of the body.

Their calling grows out of who they are as members of the people of God. That call is repeated from the earliest days until the OT closes with Malachi.

Calling in the New Testament

Our survey of the evidence in the NT constitutes the major portion of our consideration of calling language in the Bible. Again we start with the specific words for "call" and "calling," but as noted above, we also investigate other words or passages whose semantic fields overlap with our concerns.[11] We divide our investigation into two sections: the Gospels and Acts, and the NT Epistles. That way we can compare how the data emerge in narratives and in letters.

Calling in the Gospels and Acts

Since we intend to understand the nature of God's call on people's lives, we omit any discussion in the Gospels of God's call of Jesus as Messiah. Though some parallels may exist between God's call of Jesus[12] and his call of others, we leave these aside to concentrate on our main concern: the nature of God's calling in the lives of believers. First, we address texts in the Gospels that shed light on Jesus's call of his disciples or followers. What follows will not be exhaustive of all possible texts but will concentrate on those that we feel fairly and faithfully represent the evidence.

Many uses of calling language in the Gospels are not relevant to our concern. "Call" commonly means to give a name (e.g., Matt.

11. To repeat, we also assess relevant uses of terms such as "appoint," "choose/ elect," and God's "will" when they appear to point us to useful insights.

12. We get some glimpses of God's "call" of Jesus in the baptism (Matt. 3:13–17// Mark 1:9–11; 9:7; Luke 3:21–22; 9:35; John 1:29–34) and transfiguration accounts (Matt. 17:1–9//Mark 9:2–10//Luke 9:28–36), as well as other places in the Gospels. Paul also gives a theological perspective in Phil. 2:6–11 and Col. 1:15–20.

1:25 KJV). "Call" often means to summon or invite others (e.g., Matt. 2:7). We will focus on examples where Jesus issues calls to people. Early in his ministry Jesus calls the fishermen James and John, and they follow him (Matt. 4:21 par.). Jesus's mission is to call (invite) sinners to repentance (Matt. 9:13//Mark 2:17//Luke 5:32).

Jesus calls and appoints the Twelve to be his disciples (or apostles) out of the larger body of his followers (Mark 3:13–14; Luke 6:13; cf. Acts 1:2; 10:41–42). The verbs "call" and "choose" in these parallel texts seem virtually synonymous. Jesus appoints these to be with him, to preach, and to have authority to exorcise demons (see Mark 6:7). John adds that Jesus chooses the Twelve, including one who is a devil (John 6:70). Jesus chooses them to function in the role or task of apostle; no salvific sense of election is intended here, as the mention of Judas presumably makes clear. John also states that Jesus chooses and appoints the Eleven to bear fruit (John 15:16). Again, this election is not for salvation as such but to a task or life that will issue in fruit. This is Jesus's call to them. The next verse may make clear one element of the fruit intended: they are to "love each other" (15:17) despite the opposition they will face as followers of Jesus in the world (15:18–27).

In addition to the Twelve, Jesus appoints (not "calls") seventy-two followers to go two by two on a mission to proclaim the good news (Luke 10:1). Following the defection of Judas, the apostles submit to the risen Jesus their nominees to replace him. Through the casting of lots, Jesus chooses Matthias (Acts 1:24–26). In several places, the writer of Acts emphasizes that God also selects Saul/Paul to be an apostle ("chosen instrument," Acts 9:15). God chooses him to be "a light for the Gentiles" (13:47), and God appoints him to his apostolic ministry (22:10, 14; 26:16).

In addition to the eleven apostles, Matthias, and Saul, does the author of Acts provide any further insight about "calling" for those who engage in ministries? The members of the Jerusalem church appoint seven leading men full of the Holy Spirit to oversee the Jerusalem ministry of food distribution (6:5–7). One of them is Stephen, who is subsequently martyred for his testimony to Jesus. Philip performs significant ministries in Samaria and elsewhere. Luke makes no mention that God called the Seven to their ministries. We never learn how Agabus or other Christian prophets (Acts 11:27–28; 21:9–11) came to occupy those roles. Luke does not use the language of calling or divine appointment to describe their activities in the way that prominent OT prophets are described.

In Acts 13:2 we discover that the Holy Spirit instructs five prophets and teachers of the church at Antioch to "set apart for me Barnabas and Saul [two of the five] for the work to which I have *called* them" (emphasis added). Apparently, Luke envisions this as a corporate discernment of the Spirit's call of these two. Perhaps God issues this call through a prophetic word to one or more of them. Acknowledging their commission, the church sends them off. Barnabas experiences the same call to this mission as the apostle Saul. James (Jesus's half brother) leads the Jerusalem church (Acts 12:17; 15:13; 21:18), but we do not know how he came to embrace that role. Clearly, elders (along with apostles) function as leaders in the Jerusalem church at that time (15:2; 21:18). In his speech to the Ephesian church elders at Miletus, Paul affirms that God appointed them as overseers (Acts 20:17, 28; cf. 21:18), but we have no information about how any of the elders mentioned in these texts came to occupy their role. Nor do we know how Mark came to be engaged in ministry with Paul and Barnabas (Acts 12:25; 15:37, 39). No calling language occurs.

On Paul's second journey, he recruits first Silas as a companion (Acts 15:40), then Timothy (16:1–3), and eventually Luke ("we" language in 16:10 and elsewhere indicate that the author of Acts, presumably Luke, enters the narrative), but the author gives no insight about their selection apart from Paul's own decision to add them to his team.[13] On that journey they experience divine guidance at several, though not all, points directing their movements (see, e.g., Acts 16:6–10; 18:9–10). Based on a vision, Paul concludes that God has called (Gk. *proskaleō*) them to travel to Macedonia to preach there (16:9–10). We cannot consider these as normative for subsequent missionaries since divine visions rarely occur in Luke's overall depiction of Paul's movements, nor does Luke give any hint that these are regular ways in which God directs the apostle's decisions. Apollos plays a significant role in Ephesus before he moves to Achaia, but Luke gives no insight into how he arrives at his position as an evangelist and church builder or the decision to travel to Achaia (Acts 18:24–25; cf. 19:1; 1 Cor. 3:4–6). Likewise, we learn nothing about the status of Priscilla and Aquila, who instruct Apollos (18:2, 18–19, 26). No language suggests that they were called to the job of making tents (nor was Paul called to that occupation) or to the ministry roles they performed in the early churches.

Paul's extended message to the Ephesian elders at Miletus (20:17–38) provides no insight into how they came to be in that role. If Luke gives us any information about the selection of elders, it is limited to what he says about the churches that Paul planted on his first journey. Luke writes that Paul and Barnabas appointed elders in each of the churches (Acts 14:23). Beyond that human appointment, we cannot venture. We may tentatively presume that the criteria for appointing people to these roles centered on the qualifications mentioned in the selection of Joseph and Matthias to replace Judas (Acts 1:21–23) or the Seven, who are described as upright and full of faith and of the Holy Spirit, of God's grace and power, and of wisdom (Acts 6:5, 8, 10). In other words, they were men of character and spiritual

---

13. Paul gives tantalizingly few details in 1 Tim. 4:14 and 2 Tim. 1:6, perhaps pointing to some occasion when Timothy's gifts for ministry were recognized by church elders.

maturity, gifted for the roles to which they were appointed. Luke provides no basis for conjecturing that these candidates sensed a personal "call" to their role or that they needed to discover their calling.

Conclusions about Calling in the Gospels and Acts

Given the nature and function of these narrative texts, it is not surprising that apostles stand out as "called ones." As Messiah and Lord, Jesus needed to select and prepare a cadre of leaders who would carry on his mission "to seek and to save the lost" (Luke 19:10). This accounts for Jesus's appointment or selection of the Twelve, Matthias, and Paul. The Gospels report that Jesus also appointed seventy-two to engage in a short-term mission, perhaps as training for their ministries after Jesus's eventual departure. What conclusions can we draw?

First, the "call" to ministry that we find in the Gospels involves concrete or explicit words of Jesus during his earthly, pre-resurrection ministry. We never hear the "called ones" speak of a mystical or subjective sense of calling. There are no hints that they had to discern whether Jesus was calling them. Jesus verbally called them when he was physically with them. Second, in the case of Matthias, the selection came via the mechanism of lots, but the writer of Acts reports that the resurrected Jesus determined the outcome (Acts 1:23–26). In other words, the ascended Jesus made another concrete choice that was clear to the remaining eleven disciples and the others waiting in Jerusalem (the text says there were about 120 meeting in prayer; Acts 1:15).

Finally, Saul's/Paul's "call" comes through a miraculous divine intervention. Not only does Jesus get his attention with a flash of light that knocks him down, but Saul also hears Jesus's voice and is struck blind. After these demonstrative acts, Jesus sends a disciple named Ananias to explain the nature of Jesus's call on Saul's life—first to salvation and then to ministry. Paul later recounts how that conversation went: "'Brother

Saul, receive your sight!' And at that very moment I was able to see him. Then he said: 'The God of our ancestors has chosen you to know his will and to see the Righteous One and to hear words from his mouth. You will be his witness to all people of what you have seen and heard. And now what are you waiting for? Get up, be baptized and wash your sins away, calling on his name'" (Acts 22:13–16).

Saul had to make a choice when confronted with the evidence the risen Jesus communicated to him directly and audibly (the men with Saul also heard the sound; Acts 9:7) on the road to Damascus and through the words of Ananias in his house on Straight Street in Damascus. Whatever reflections or ruminations Saul may have engaged in before these events, the narrator makes clear that Saul's call was not some subjective experience discerned only by him (i.e., he "felt called"). We find an objective appointment by Jesus himself. What's more, as with the Twelve and Matthias, this is an *apostolic* appointment and therefore, we insist, a special case. We have no reason to conclude that these direct appointments by Jesus constitute a paradigm for the call of subsequent leaders. Nothing normative for us emerges from these instances. Of course, we cannot deny that God may choose to select someone and miraculously convey his special appointment to serve him. But it appears that these instances are the exception rather than the norm. The biblical texts themselves give us no warrant to expect such exceptions, and we should not put a burden on ourselves or others to wait expectantly for some explicit word from Jesus calling us or them to a specific ministry.

In Acts we found numerous "leaders" functioning in various capacities in connection with the emerging churches. In this category are the Seven, Agabus and other prophets, elders, and Paul's companions in ministry. We saw no evidence of specific language indicating that they discerned a divine calling for their roles or tasks. If anything, they assumed their roles because they were gifted and spiritually qualified people. Others recognized that they possessed these qualities and assigned them to their positions. The repetition of this pattern underscores that this is a normative principle.

Luke uses calling language to identify the Spirit's guidance in Paul's decision to travel to Macedonia (Acts 16:10). God gave Paul a vision during the night; Paul interpreted this as a divine call to preach in Europe. As with other visionary experiences that we surveyed in Acts, this "call" fits the category of an isolated, special, miraculous intervention by which God clearly conveys specific directions or instructions. Saul's experience on the Damascus road fits here as well. With a blinding light, the voice from heaven, and the words of the disciple Ananias, God communicated directly to Saul.

We think it would be unreasonable to consider these examples as normative. God certainly *may* confront someone through extraordinary means—including a vision or other form of communication—to call them to a specific location. We have no warrant to deny that God may issue such an unmistakable call or appointment for ministry today. But two important points seem evident: (1) we dare not conclude from these isolated examples that they are normative, and (2) we cannot generalize from these very specific and foundational *apostolic* appointments[14] and assume that they provide a normal or expected pattern for how God calls people today. Rather, the examples of wise discernment that leaders exercised to determine qualified ministry candidates and to appoint them to ministry opportunities points us to what is normative.

Calling in the Epistles

When we survey the NT Epistles, we find a wide array of references that have significance for our project. The apostolic

---

14. Paul considers the apostles as first among the foundational pillars of the church. See 1 Cor. 12:28; Eph. 2:20; 3:5; 4:11; cf. 2 Pet. 3:2; Jude 17.

authors often use "calling" and "election" language for the "call to salvation" or "election to salvation." As we will see, the call to salvation, to membership in the body of Christ, is foundational to how calling language is used of those who are Christ's followers. This is crucial for gaining the central meaning of calling language. Believers are the ones whom God has "called" (Rom. 9:24). Quoting Hosea, Paul goes on to affirm: "I will *call* them 'my people' who are not my people; and I will *call* her 'my loved one' who is not my loved one" (Rom. 9:25, emphasis added). Our task, then, is to study the nature of God's *call* on his people's lives. For clarity, we will separate the data into several categories. Seeing these data in this way will enable us to draw the most useful conclusions.

God Appoints Paul

In many of his letters, Paul affirms that God chose, set apart, or appointed him to be an apostle.[15] Sometimes Paul affirms his appointment in unique terms: he was given the "grace" of apostleship.[16] In other places, he claims to be a "called apostle" based on the will of God.[17] In other words, Paul believed he had a divine vocation. God appointed Paul to preach and to defend the gospel.[18] At one point, Paul claims that God assigned to him an arena of ministry (2 Cor. 10:13). These Pauline references parallel what we discovered in the Gospels and Acts to be God's appointment of apostles. God calls apostles to function in that specific role.[19]

---

15. Examples include Rom. 1:1; 1 Cor. 9:16–17; Gal. 1:15; Phil. 1:16; 1 Tim. 1:1, 12; Titus 1:3. See also "election," Acts 9:15; "command/choose/assign/appoint" in 13:47; 22:10, 14; 26:16. Several other letter writers simply affirm their apostolic status or credentials for writing without claiming explicitly a call or appointment: James 1:1; 1 Pet. 1:1; 2 Pet. 1:1; 2 John 1; 3 John 1; Jude 1; Rev. 1:1.

16. Rom. 12:3; 15:15–16; 1 Cor. 15:10; Eph. 3:7–8.

17. Rom. 1:1; 1 Cor. 1:1; 2 Cor. 1:1; Eph. 1:1; Col. 1:1; 2 Tim. 1:1.

18. 1 Cor. 9:16–17; Phil. 1:16; 1 Tim. 2:7; 2 Tim. 1:11.

19. For a pointed analysis of the uses of "call" in Paul's Letters, see W. Klein, "Paul's Use of *kalein*."

God Appoints People to Serve Him

In addition to Paul, God appointed others to serve him in various tasks. God appointed Abraham as a father to many nations, adding, "the God who gives life to the dead and *calls* into being things that were not" (Rom. 4:17, emphasis added). God called or appointed Aaron as high priest (Heb. 5:4). God appointed Jacob (rather than Esau) to continue the line of what would become the nation Israel (Rom. 9:11–13). God is the one who makes these "calls" (Rom. 9:12). God appointed Pharaoh for his divine purposes, to allow the Jews to escape Egypt (Rom. 9:17, 21). God gifts people to serve him—a very general "grace" for service, not specific persons to specific jobs (Rom. 12:6; 1 Cor. 12:28; Eph. 4:7). Persons often find their role in ministries that particularly employ their gifts, such as evangelist, pastor, or teacher (Eph. 4:11). In other words, God grants to people spiritual gifts so that they qualify to serve in roles or functions for building up the body of Christ. Paul never says that God calls specific people for particular church positions or offices. God appoints human (governmental) authority—again a seemingly general action, not a specific emperor or governor (Rom. 13:1). And as he did with Paul, God appointed Apollos as a foundational minister for the Corinthian churches (1 Cor. 3:4).

As to specific persons besides himself, Paul's uses range from God's choice of the patriarchs of Israel, to Pharaoh, to Apollos. It seems that the patriarchs and Pharaoh belong in a special or unique category, parallel to apostles—ones especially designated as foundational in the progress of the history of salvation. Governments have a calling to serve God by promoting the common good and punishing wrongdoers. Probably Apollos fits in the category of those to whom God gives graces that enable them to serve the church, such as elders and Paul's various ministry associates in Acts. Paul never hints that they have any special "vocational call" to a specific place or job; rather, they have an obligation to serve God, which they fulfill in specific locations and functions with their gifts and the needs they perceive. This obligation grows out of their "calling in Christ," though we must await further investigation before we explore how that works.

We return to our discussion of the office or role of elders since several NT letters acknowledge their presence. In 1 Timothy, Paul identifies elders who direct the affairs of the church and goes on to discuss several matters about their oversight (1 Tim. 5:17, 19). His instructions to Titus imply a similar leadership role (Titus 1:5–6). Most likely the title "overseers" (Gk. *episkopoi*) is another way to describe these leaders (see Phil. 1:1; 1 Tim. 3:1; Titus 1:7).[20] James counsels his sick readers to call the elders of the church to pray for them (James 5:14). Peter instructs elders in the churches to lead well (1 Pet. 5:1–3). The one who writes 2 John and 3 John identifies himself as "the elder," which may indicate his church office or be only an honorific title like the "elder statesman" (2 John 1; 3 John 1). To the office of elder/overseer we must add "deacon" since Paul in several places refers to them as leaders: Phoebe (Rom. 16:1); at Ephesus (1 Tim. 3:8–13); and at Philippi (Phil. 1:1).

Conclusions about Calling in the Epistles

What insights do these passages provide? In places, leadership roles are simply assumed; organized churches require leaders, and we may well identify several layers of leaders, if not a hierarchy. Did the leaders need to be "called" to their positions? We find no calling language in these passages. What little insight we have comes from Paul's discussions of the qualifications for overseers and deacons in 1 Timothy and Titus. First, Paul affirms that one can aspire or desire to become an overseer (1 Tim. 3:1). But aspiration alone (or may we add for our purposes, a subjective sense of "calling") is not enough, for Paul immediately provides a list of

20. Scholars debate the possible ways to understand the relationship between overseers and elders, but the outcome of this has no bearing on our concerns. They function as church leaders, as do "deacons."

qualities that a suitable candidate must possess (1 Tim. 3:2–7; cf. Titus 1:6–9). Similarly, deacons must meet certain qualifications of character and experience (1 Tim. 3:8–12). His mention of the need to test candidates before they serve (3:10) suggests that the church has the obligation to scrutinize potential candidates for the offices of overseer/elder and deacon. Paul never mentions that they need to have a sense of "calling" or some divine word appointing them to service. Some may want to lead, but the congregation must verify aspiring candidates' credentials and determine their suitability.

Can we detect anything normative for us in this section? These are descriptive passages. God sovereignly chooses the patriarchs, Pharaoh, and governing authorities. God gives spiritual gifts that outfit his people to serve him, and that is precisely the normative component for us: God graciously equips his people. Biblical passages amply affirm that God gives gifts for his people to serve in the church (e.g., Rom. 12:4–8; 1 Cor. 12; 14; Eph. 4:7–13; 1 Pet. 4:10–11). Testing potential church leaders for their suitability seems normative, for its application goes beyond the specific situation that Paul dealt with in Ephesus when writing to Timothy. Therefore, meeting qualifications is also normative, as we saw with the appointment of the Seven in Acts 6: full of the Spirit and wisdom. All told, the qualifications center mainly on character, orthodoxy, and experience, though we do not presume that 1 Timothy and Titus provide exhaustive criteria. *Where* leaders serve has no normativity about it. The most Paul said about locations for service comes in some final words in Romans: "It has always been my ambition to preach the gospel where Christ was not known, so that I would not be building on someone else's foundation" (Rom. 15:20). Notice that he speaks of his own ambition, not God's call. In the conversion reports in Acts, God calls Paul to preach to Gentiles, a very general area of service. A feeling of being "called" appears nowhere. The imperative to use one's gifts for the common good is the normative obligation.

Finding a place that provides an opportunity to exercise our gifts and desiring to do so there provides the foundation for ministry. But is there any truly normative type of call? Stay tuned.

God Calls His People to Be

Up to this point in our survey of the NT evidence, we have concentrated on individuals. We have discovered only a few principles as normative for our lives as followers of Christ. As we will now see, the corporate understanding of calling predominates in the NT and, we will argue, gives clearer focus to our essential normativity question. Christians are called to *be*. But what does that entail? Let us review the evidence.

In a cluster of texts in Paul's writings, he affirms that God calls his people (to be) his *holy ones*, or saints. That is how God designates them; that is their status or position before God. Paul affirms that the Roman Christians are "called to be his [God's] holy ones" (Rom. 1:6–7, our trans.), called of Jesus Christ, or as most translations put it, "called to belong to Jesus Christ." He repeats this status in his description of the Corinthian believers as "called to be his holy people" (Gk. *klētois hagiois* = called saints; 1 Cor. 1:2). The Galatian believers are, in short, ones whom God has called (Gal. 5:8). God's calling comes "through [the] gospel" (2 Thess. 2:14). This repetition in manifold texts suggests a *normative* descriptor; the called constitute God's people, his holy ones. Every believer has this calling, for they belong to Christ.

The author of Hebrews also applies the terms "calling" (Gk. *klēsis*) and "holy" to the entire body of believers: the holy brothers and sisters who share in a heavenly calling (Heb. 3:1). They all possess this status. To say that the readers have a "calling" is another way of referring to them as believers. Jude also names his readers as "those who have been called" (Jude 1). They are loved and "kept safe" (NRSV). In his Apocalypse, John also employs this blanket label for believers; along with being "called," they are Jesus's chosen and faithful followers (Rev. 17:14).

Adding an additional nuance, Paul affirms that the believers are called into fellowship with Christ, into the community of the body of Jesus Christ, the church (1 Cor. 1:9). God has called the Corinthian believers into fellowship (Gk. *koinōnia*) with his Son, Jesus Christ. Again, this underscores the corporate nature of God's call, which entails the church's corporate identity in union with Christ and all other believers. Peter affirms that God "called" believers to his eternal glory in Christ (1 Pet. 5:10). This is their identity and future hope.

God Calls People to Lives That Reflect Their Identity as "Called Ones"

Given their identity, God calls his people to live in ways that reflect this calling. In other words, their status or identity as "called ones" dictates how they must live. Paul makes this point in several texts. They are to live peacefully or in peace (1 Cor. 7:15; Col. 3:15). Grace rather than law keeping must characterize their lives (Gal. 1:6). That is, God's gracious calling of them implies that they are free from certain demands of the law (Gal. 5:13–14). In addition, God's people are called to live in ways that reflect the hope they have in Christ (Eph. 1:18). More generally, they must live lives that are worthy of this high calling or status in Christ (Eph. 4:1, 4; 1 Thess. 2:12; 2 Thess. 1:11). Since they possess this high and lofty status as God's called ones, they ought to conduct their lives in ways that demonstrate this identity. On the ethical front, Christians are called to avoid impurity and to embrace holiness (Gk. *hagiasmos*: 1 Thess. 4:7; cf. Rom. 6:19, 22). Believers have a "holy [Gk. *hagios*] calling" (2 Tim. 1:9 NRSV). That is, their identity as saints or holy ones implies that their lives should exhibit their separation unto God to accomplish his purposes in and through them.

The *corporate* nature of their calling has important implications. No doubt Paul's criticism of the abuse of the Lord's Supper by the Corinthian Christians grew out of his view of the unity of the church, which must be demonstrated in their behavior toward one another (1 Cor. 10:17; 11:18–34). They are one body. Following Paul's appeal that believers "live a life worthy of the calling you have received" (Eph. 4:1), he adds, "Be completely humble and gentle; be patient, bearing with one another in love. Make every effort to keep the unity of the Spirit through the bond of peace. There is one body and one Spirit, just as you were called to one hope when you were called; one Lord, one faith, one baptism; one God and Father of all, who is over all and through all and in all" (Eph. 4:2–6). A corporate calling requires corporate efforts to become what they are in Christ.

These verses are crucial for our understanding of calling. Following God's call must reflect our connection to all others in the church. Affixed to our calling are the following: humility, gentleness, patience, love for each other, unity, peace, one hope, all within the framework of one Lord, faith, baptism, and God. Finally, Christians should live in ways that signify that they are called to eternal life (1 Tim. 6:12). In Paul's eloquent words, "So we fix our eyes not on what is seen, but on what is unseen, since what is seen is temporary, but what is unseen is eternal" (2 Cor. 4:18). Our calling in Christ lifts our focus to eternal realities.

Likewise, Peter urges his readers to demonstrate in their behavior their identity in Christ. Holiness emerges as crucial for him as well. He argues that because the holy God has called (Gk. *kaleō*) believers, they are to be holy in all they do (1 Pet. 1:15; cf. 2:9). Since they are saints (holy ones), they must demonstrate holiness in their behavior. Their calling may well entail suffering, following the example of their Lord Jesus (2:20). Their calling may require repaying evil with blessing (3:9). That parallels what we find in 2 Peter, where the writer urges his readers to "make every effort to confirm your calling [Gk. *klēsis*] and election" (1:10). He lists a crescendo of qualities that ought to characterize those who possess this divine calling (see 1:5–9). All his readers possess this "calling"; their obligation is to confirm it in their actions.

One text in Paul's writings seems to be an outlier: 1 Cor. 7:20. Many discussions of "calling" over the years have sought to make much of this one use. There he says, "Each person should remain in the situation [literally, "calling"; Gk. *klēsis*] they were in when God called [Gk. *kaleō*] them." Believers obtain salvation when God calls them; that is their saved status, as we have seen. Here Paul uses the noun "calling" uniquely to refer to a situation (NIV, CEB, CSB) in life (NET), a condition (NRSV, ESV, NASB), or a state (NABRE, NJB) the Corinthian believers occupied when the divine call to salvation came. He lists such situations as circumcision, uncircumcision, slavery, and freedom. That is, when they embraced Christ in salvation, some of his readers were circumcised, others were not. Some were slaves, others were not. Some were married, and some were single. Here he speaks uniquely of these as "callings."

Despite what Luther argued, all commentators and English translations agree that we should not equate these "callings" with jobs: they were common situations or circumstances of life that these people occupied when they embraced Christ.[21] Here's the million-dollar question: Does Paul intend to affirm here that every person has a specific "calling" from God that amounts to their current situation?[22] And if so, does this mean, as Luther and a few others have concluded, that after becoming a Christian, believers should never seek to change their situation, for it is ordained by God? No on all fronts. As we said, this is a unique text. "Calling" here is simply a nontechnical way of saying that people in various walks of life or circumstances become believers. Paul's point is that believers should not seek to change their circumstances if by remaining in them they can serve Christ more faithfully. Paul is not elevating a specific circumstance (and certainly not a job) to the status of a *divine calling*. "Paul's point

---

21. This parallels what Paul said in 1 Cor. 1:26: "Think of what you were when you were called."

22. We saw in our historical surveys that many have opted for this very understanding.

is not that God calls people to a vocation or state, but that he calls people to salvation while they are in some existing calling (situation, circumstance)."[23]

Conclusions about God's Calling

In the NT Epistles, "calling" is the status or position of those who are in Christ, in fellowship with Christ. God has named (called) this body as his own. This calling is corporate, one that enjoins believers to exult in their status or identity as God's special possession, those who anticipate the future hope of glory. As the temple of the Holy Spirit, together they can live in ways that reflect that they are "in Christ."[24] This is a call to community, for God's people constitute a corporate entity that exists as a body, not as isolated individuals. Christians are the body of Christ. That is who they are; that is their calling.

Consequently, every believer has a calling, or vocation if you will. But in light of the evidence we have uncovered, this must be framed carefully. The believer's "call" resides not in a task (or a job, or a passion, or the like) or in a position in life but in the values and practices one exhibits as a "called" person in the church and the world. Who believers *are* in Christ constitutes their calling, not where they live, their job, or their station in life. None of these traits describes their calling. Their calling is to be in Christ and to live accordingly.

Determining normativity proves simple at this point. All Christians are called by virtue of their membership in the body of Christ. Calling exists not in their job, ministry, station, marital status, an office in the church or government, or any other circumstance. Calling is not something to search for or to pray for guidance in finding. Of course, believers can fail to live up to their

---

23. W. Klein, *New Chosen People*, 184.
24. Due to the critical nature of this "in Christ" construct, we will devote a later section to unpacking its significance for our understanding of calling.

calling, and that accounts for the apostolic authors' appeals for their readers to put on their identity in Christ. To repeat Paul's words, "I urge you to live a life worthy of the calling you have received" (Eph. 4:1). But no believers need be unsure of their calling or uncertain about what that call entails. Their identity in Christ confirms their vocation.

God's Will for People

Often in popular discussions about the topic of call or vocation, the issue of the will of God surfaces. Serious Christians ask, What is God's will for my life? Clearly for many people, this overlaps with the question of "call." Answering the question "Is God calling me to something specific?" may be equivalent in their minds to finding God's will.[25] Is it God's will that someone be a pastor or missionary? Does God will (or desire) that some serve him as praise-band members? What about real estate brokers, software engineers, day-care workers, hotel maids, or assembly-plant operators? Does God desire some to function in specific occupations or roles, to be married or to remain single? If so, are these callings? If not, has God's will any role to play in the choices believers make? To answer these kinds of questions, we need to investigate how the NT uses the concept of God's will in relation to people. We will use a convenient breakdown for surveying the relevant occurrences of God's will. In what follows, we will not attempt to be exhaustive but will survey enough texts to clarify how the terms for God's "will" occur.

God's Will as What God Wishes or Desires

We saw above that God "calls" people to live in ways that conform to his claim on their lives as his "called" people. We might

25. For a useful discussion on finding God's will, see Friesen, *Decision Making and the Will of God.*

say that God "invites" people to live in peace, grace, freedom, hope, purity, and holiness—though we dare not consider these optional. Paul uses God's "will" in this sense as well, as what God wishes or desires of his people. Jesus urges his disciples to pray that God's "will [Gk. *thelēma*] be done on earth as it is in heaven" (Matt. 6:10). We realize all too well that God's will is not always done, but we ought to pray for it and implement it as we are able. Quoting Hosea 6:6, Jesus affirms that God "desires [Gk. *thelō*] mercy" (Matt. 9:13). It is possible to choose what God wills (Gk. *thelō*) or to choose another way (Isa. 56:4 LXX). The Lord delights in ("wills," Gk. *thelō*) such virtues as kindness, justice, and righteousness (Jer. 9:24 [9:23 LXX]).

Paul urges his readers to "be transformed by the renewing of your mind. Then you will be able to test and approve what God's *will* is—his good, pleasing and perfect *will* [Gk. *thelēma*]" (Rom. 12:2, emphasis added). Spiritual renewal and transformation are requisites for discerning God's will. A renewed mind is equipped to discern God's will based on a sanctified capacity to think spiritually. Following on from that, it is God's "will" (Gk. *thelēma*) that believers "be sanctified" (Gk. *hagiosmos*), or set apart—specifically, that they abstain from immorality (1 Thess. 4:3). This corresponds to our earlier findings about God's call to holiness. Also in that letter, Paul affirms that it is God's will (Gk. *thelēma*) that his readers engage in rejoicing, continual prayer, and constant thankfulness (1 Thess. 5:18). Peter encourages obedience to human authorities and doing good as God's will (1 Pet. 2:15). Many of these virtues that God wills or desires correspond to what we have seen as God's *call* for purity and holiness. How God calls people to live corresponds to his will for them. Clearly the meanings of the terms overlap in such uses.

In the prophecy of Jonah, it appears that God intended to destroy the wicked people of Nineveh. He sent Jonah to proclaim that message, which he eventually did (Jon. 1:2; 3:4). But the Ninevites repented, hoping that God would relent and spare them

(3:5–9). In fact, when God saw their repentance, "God changed his mind about the calamity that he had said he would bring upon them; and he did not do it" (Jon. 3:10 NRSV). Though God had announced his intention to destroy Nineveh, apparently that intent or "will" was conditional and so was not implemented. The Ninevites met God's condition of repentance from their sins, and God withheld his judgment.

Jesus says, "Whoever does God's will [Gk. *thelēma*] is my brother and sister and mother" (Mark 3:35). Certainly, some do God's will, and others do not. Human response to what God desires determines their spiritual standing as members of Jesus's family. Jesus desired ("willed," Gk. *thelō*) to gather the Jerusalemites together, but they "were not willing" (Matt. 23:37). The Jewish people set their wills against Jesus's will. The words of the apostles likewise point to a central desire of God: his desire to save all sinful humans. Paul writes that God *wills* (Gk. *thelō*) that all people find his salvation (1 Tim. 2:4). Peter confirms this: "God is not *wanting* [Gk. *boulomai*] anyone to perish, but [wants] everyone to come to repentance" (2 Pet. 3:9). To repeat, these are examples of what God wishes or desires, but God's will may or may not occur since it depends on human response or obedience.[26]

God's Will as What God Sovereignly Determines

In contrast to the preceding category, God's will at times specifies what he determines or implements unconditionally. James asserts, "Of his own will [Gk. *boulomai*] he brought us forth by the word of truth" (1:18 ESV). Paul attributes many aspects of God's provision of salvation to this divine and sovereign will. It was God's will (Gk. *thelēma*) that Jesus give himself for our sins (Gal. 1:4). God's purpose (Gk. *prothesis*) accounts for his "calling" people to salvation (Rom. 8:28–30). Indeed, God's will or purpose

---

26. For other examples of this conditional will of God, see Eph. 6:6; Heb. 10:36; 1 John 2:17.

stands behind salvation itself (1 Cor. 1:21; Eph. 1:9; 2 Tim. 1:9). Jesus affirms that he "gives life to whom he will [Gk. *thelō*]" (John 5:21 ESV). God's will is behind every action that God performs, whether it is showing mercy or hardening (Rom. 9:18; Gk. *thelō*), or showing love or wrath. God's purposes (Gk. *prothesis*) that proceed from the counsel of his will (Gk. *thelēma*) account for what God then predestines (Eph. 1:11).

Seen negatively, God refused to remove Paul's thorn despite his ardent prayers (2 Cor. 12:7–9). Paul acknowledged that God was sovereign over his physical situation; God effected his will by denying Paul's petition. In a similar vein, despite three requests from his Son, God did not spare Jesus from the cross, and Jesus affirmed, "Not as I will, but as you will [Gk. *thelō*]" (Matt. 26:39). At times God effectually implements his will; what God wills happens (see discussion below).

Once the nature of God's will is understood in this way, we must acknowledge a contingency when we assert our own will or make our plans. The point of Jesus's parable of the rich fool hinges on a common human oversight. The fool assumed he was in charge of his fate, but God had other plans (Luke 12:20). James's classic phrase "If the Lord wills [Gk. *thelō*]" (James 4:15 ESV) locates human plans within the overall rubric of God's will. Paul recognizes this contingency in his plans to visit Corinth ("if the Lord is willing," 1 Cor. 4:19; "if the Lord permits," 16:7) and Rome ("by God's will," Rom. 1:10). When his will is understood in this sense, it would be the height of presumption to think that human plans can overrule what God determines.

God's Will as What God Allows Other Agents to Perform

We add a final category that accounts for instances when God's will *allows* actions that God neither desires nor performs. In fact, God may well oppose actions, events, or people but nevertheless chooses to allow them to occur or proceed. Given the way God has sovereignly set up our world—he is indeed "in charge"—he allows events or actions to occur without his active role, even though they go against what God prefers or desires. For example, under his sovereign oversight—how God wills the world to be— God allowed Adam and Eve to rebel through disobedience. As noted above, though God is "*not willing* that any perish" (2 Pet. 3:9 KJV, emphasis added), the biblical evidence shows that some people do reject God's salvation and suffer the consequences. God wills that none perish but allows people to reject his will. Peter says that God allows ("if it is God's will [Gk. *thelō, thelēma*]," 1 Pet. 3:17) suffering to afflict his people, even though human enemies are responsible "according to the will [Gk. *thelēma*] of God" (4:19 KJV). Surely God does not desire that his people undergo suffering inflicted by their enemies, but he wills to allow it. When preaching at Lystra, Paul explained that God "let all nations go their own way" (Acts 14:16), tolerating their "ignorance" (17:30).

To take a final example, Jesus cites Pilate's murder of some Galileans and the collapse of a tower in Siloam that claimed eighteen lives (Luke 13:1, 4). Some things happen due to human sin or malfeasance; natural disasters result in loss of life and property. God wills to allow such events in our fallen world. Texts such as these and others do not imply that God caused Adam's rebellion or that he prevents some from obtaining salvation, causes his enemies to afflict believers, produces people's ignorance, or causes all natural disasters (despite the fact that insurance companies call them "acts of God").[27] Rather, we learn that in God's oversight of the world he has made, he wills to allow these kinds of actions and events.

Some texts defy an easy categorization. To cite an OT example, the Deuteronomist asserts that if any Israelites violate the terms of

---

27. We do not mean to imply, however, that God never intervenes in human affairs when it suits his purposes. For an obvious example, in judgment God visited a natural disaster upon the cities of Sodom and Gomorrah (Gen. 19:23–25).

God's covenant with them, "the LORD will never be willing [Gk. *thelō*] to forgive them; his wrath and zeal will burn against them" (Deut. 29:20a [29:19a LXX]). The verses that follow this threat (29:20b–29) seem to indicate that God's judgments against these covenant breakers will be severe and that there will be no reprieve. But we may ask, What happens if they later repent? Would God relent and forgive as he did the Ninevites in Jonah's time? To take a NT text, in Matt. 18:14 Jesus says that God is not willing (Gk. *thelēma*) that any of these little ones (those who believe in Jesus; 18:6) perish. While avoiding the theological controversies here, we can see the possibility of two options: (1) God's will may refer to his *desire* that may or may not come to pass: some little ones may perish because the misdeeds of others lead them astray; or (2) God has *determined* it to be so and enforces his will so that no little ones will ever perish.

Conclusions about God's Will

How does God's will impact the issue of his "call" upon believers? We have seen three basic senses for understanding the nature of God's will. Let's take each of them in order. First, God desires certain behaviors, values, and beliefs to characterize his people. These are God's will for believers. We, therefore, have an obligation to pursue them, for God desires that we do so. The Beatitudes in the Sermon on the Mount describe those whom God blesses; they flourish because they live as God wills for them to live (Matt. 5:3–12). God is pleased when his people allow his Spirit to transform their lives, when they pursue holiness, when they pray, and when they do good to all—among the many virtues we could list. So those who desire to find God's will for their lives need only read the Bible carefully to learn the kind of life that pleases God.

Notice, however, that under this category of God's will (or call), God does not enforce godliness. People can lie to the Holy

Spirit, they may quench the Holy Spirit, and they can reject God's will for them. After presenting the gospel to the Jews in Antioch of Pisidia, Paul said, "We had to speak the word of God to you first. Since you reject it and do not consider yourselves worthy of eternal life, we now turn to the Gentiles" (Acts 13:46). God wanted them to be saved, but they thwarted God's will for them.

Second, God sometimes acts determinatively and unconditionally to accomplish his will. When God's will is enacted in this sense, people need not wonder if they have discovered God's will for themselves: it is or will be done. In this determinative sense, when God wills a specific action to impact a person, they have no recourse; it will happen. God created the universe, and it was so. God caused the flood. We might even venture that God sovereignly confronted Saul on his way to Damascus. There was no uncertainty about his call to apostleship; yet even after that divine encounter, Paul still needed to embrace his call on God's terms: repent and believe (Acts 22:16). God determinatively apprehends some for his service (e.g., Abraham, Pharaoh, and Judas). We must allow, therefore, that God may single out some people for special service.

For another example, when God willed that Ananias and Sapphira be struck dead for their deceit and hypocrisy, they fell dead (Acts 5:1–10). When God willed that Paul would testify about Jesus in Rome (Acts 23:11), no human attempts to end his life prematurely succeeded. He was bulletproof! Believers must make their plans as wisdom demands and as Paul did on his many journeys, but they should plan with the realization that they and their plans are contingent. God's will may overrule theirs, and God may turn their plans upside down. James's counsel is crucial: when making plans, we must always say "If the Lord wills" (James 4:15 ESV).

We discovered a third way to understand God's will: what he allows. In God's oversight of the world, he chooses to allow human actions, events, or circumstances that he does not directly cause or desire, things that might anger him. What might this contribute to our understanding of God's "call" of people? God allows things that displease him (e.g., human sin; the death of people due to earthquakes). We inhabit a hostile world, where the enemies of God—human as well as "spiritual forces of evil in the heavenly realms" (Eph. 6:12)—have freedom to oppose God's people and their plans. This should give us every incentive to ensure that we carefully follow what God has called us to be, the people of God—that we be strong in the Lord and put on the armor of God, as Paul urges his readers in Eph. 6:10–18. But there are no guarantees that we will accomplish all we desire or propose.

Christians pursue God's calling against the backdrop of the church's enemies, whether human or supernatural, but many vagaries of life also confront Christians on a regular basis. We live in a culture of relentless change, where new circumstances or challenges present themselves with unsettling regularity. Jobs are eliminated; bodies get old; marriages disintegrate; new industries emerge; job transfers are required; health challenges devastate savings; viruses emerge; and the list goes on and on. We wrote these words amid the COVID-19 pandemic, which upset the lives of billions of people and took the lives of millions worldwide.

We need a secure anchor in a world in flux. We are convinced that a robust concept of calling can fortify Christians to live as God intended—even when things are happening around us that neither we nor God may will or desire. If we pursue our calling as the people of God, we put ourselves in the best position to make good decisions and form plans that honor God amid our trials. We cannot control the actions of others or prevent what life may deal us, but we can be spiritually "transformed" (Rom. 12:1–2) so that we respond in ways that honor God's call for us to be his people. We are called to be faithful to our calling—not to a life of fulfillment and ease, or to the job of our dreams, or to success as our world understands it. God calls us to pursue God's will in the first sense above, faithfully living out those qualities that God fondly desires for his people.

Having concluded our analysis of the biblical evidence for the uses of "calling," we are ready to compare these results to the ways calling language has been used throughout history and in our contemporary world. We turn to that task in the next chapter.

4

Cross-Examining the Uses of Calling Language

Let us review what we have learned thus far. In chapter 1 we observed the bewildering range of uses of the term "calling" in the last fifty years or so. We saw the potential upsides as well as downsides of many of these uses. In chapter 2, we engaged in a historical study to see how our key terms were employed by writers since the founding of the church up to the middle of the last century. That survey confirmed that Christian writers have employed "calling" in specific but often contrasting ways. There is no copyright on the word "calling" to ensure that everyone uses it with the same shared definition!

But this, of course, is true of all words. Words cover what linguists call a semantic field: virtually all words have a range of meaning and are used with varying senses in different contexts. Take the word "trunk." If we asked you to define the word "trunk" in the sentence "What is the largest trunk you have ever seen?" you could not unless we identified the context for you. Is this large trunk at the zoo, in an automobile showroom, in a forest, or in a men's swimwear catalog (for those who still call them "swim trunks"). We recognize that it is a fallacy to imagine that a word has a "root meaning" independent of context.[1] What does this have to do with our topic and the key word "calling"?

First, we cannot complain that there is a range of uses among the sources we have examined. People use words to convey their meaning, even if others use the same word to convey a different meaning. But it is one thing to say that a word has a range of meaning; it is quite another to say that we can use a word to mean anything we want in any context we want. If we want others to understand what we are saying, we must use words with their agreed-upon meanings. So while we have ample evidence that "calling" has a range of meanings today and throughout history, we cannot import one of the meanings of calling (what it means in one context) and insert that meaning into another context. "Trunk" can mean a storage space in the rear of a car,[2] but we cannot employ that sense when describing an elephant's nose or a giant redwood tree.

In chapter 3 we engaged in an important biblical survey. The reason for this is simple: we believe the Bible's uses will help us address the problem of multiple meanings and contexts. What is the range of meanings the biblical writers employ? Which of those meanings is used in which contexts? If we can determine some normative meanings for "calling" in different contexts, we can apply them to the confusing uses of calling today. When writers today urge readers to find their "calling" or to embrace their call to whatever occupation they find themselves in (whether pastor, programmer, or truck driver),[3] does this line up with how the biblical writers use the term?

---

1. On the study of words, see W. Klein, Blomberg, and Hubbard, *Introduction to Biblical Interpretation*, 323–44.

2. Our friends in the UK refer to this storage space as a "boot." So they must distinguish between that storage space and footwear rather than between a tree and an elephant's nose.

3. Recall chap. 1 above.

How the Bible Uses Calling Language

First, we need to sort out the meanings in the biblical texts we surveyed in chapter 3. In the OT, all the calling uses pertain to "cultic" vocations in Israel (not to secular jobs), to what we might readily term "ministries." God called the patriarchs, national leaders (such as Moses and Joshua), kings, prophets, and priests to serve in their unique roles in the founding and history of Israel as a theocracy. But these are not normative appointments that apply to us today; we cannot claim that these calls establish specific and ongoing categories or vocations beyond historical Israel that continue in the church today. In other words, God's call on these leaders was particular to that time and nation. For example, God's calling of Abram to found the nation of Israel cannot be used today to assert that God calls an individual to plant a church. The biblical text gives no justification for such an application of the story. Furthermore, only with Jeremiah (1:4–8) and Isaiah (49:1) do we find any hint that their appointments as prophets were callings that they were uniquely created to do or be—from their birth, as it were. The corporate calling of the nation Israel to obedience, service, and witness is no doubt normative for all Israelites, and as we will see, these values are normative for the people of God in any era. We can affirm this because the NT imposes these same demands on the church.

We see similar results in the Gospels and Acts. Jesus's call of the twelve disciples (apostles) parallels God's call of leaders in ancient Israel. That is, Jesus calls specific individuals for a particular task or role—including Judas, who betrayed him. In some instances, the writers further specify some functions that these disciples or apostles will perform, such as preaching or exorcising demons. Jesus calls Paul to his apostolic role to preach to the Gentiles. The call to apostleship, however, is not normative for the ongoing church. The apostolic age concluded in the first century. No writers of the NT Epistles provide for an ongoing office of "apostle" that extends beyond Jesus's circle and to which God might call people today. In addition to the calls we have described, Jesus calls or invites sinners to repent. Certainly that call is normative; every person can say, in effect, "Jesus calls me to repent and follow him."

While the specific call to be an apostle is not normative, we concluded on the basis of some NT imperatives that the tasks assigned to the apostles are extended to all Christ-followers. In fact, even within the Gospels, Jesus appoints the seventy-two to preach the good news (Luke 10:1). Thus, while the apostles are to preach and bear fruit, those expectations extend to all disciples. The author of Acts also records that the Holy Spirit called Paul and Barnabas to a church-planting ministry, and God later called Paul to move to a different location for ministry. But Acts gives no support for considering these specific *interventions* as normative for the ongoing planting of churches or for determining potential geographical locations for mission work. Typically, Paul made his own decisions about routes to take or towns to evangelize. Paralleling the OT evidence concerning Israel's leaders, Jesus's call of the apostles gives no warrant for claiming that Jesus also calls individuals to specific roles, whether pastors, missionaries, or fund managers.

In the Epistles, God's call of *individuals* essentially replicates what we found in the OT and the Gospels/Acts. The writers affirm that God appointed Paul, Abraham, Aaron, Jacob, Pharaoh, and Apollos. These men had special functions for specific times or tasks in the progress of redemption; we can glean no sense of normativity for what God or Christ did in calling them. We did, however, discover two normative principles: (1) God graciously equips people to serve in the church and the world, and (2) Christ gifts the church with leadership offices or roles (but does not issue specific "calls" to those who fill those roles), though these may overlap with the next category, God's corporate calling.

The dominant use of calling language in the Epistles is corporate: God calls his people in Christ. Many calling texts point to the church's *identity*: the church constitutes Christ's body, God's holy ones or saints, his people, his loved ones. Together believers have a holy calling; in fact, they are the "called ones." Beyond identity, calling language addresses their *character*, or what God calls them to become because of their identity in Christ. For example, they are to live in peace, in grace, in freedom from the law, in hope, in ways that are worthy of their calling (identity), in holiness without impurity, in unity, in light of eternity, and as ones who bless others—even their persecutors. The language of what God *wills* for his people merely reinforces these virtuous behaviors and character traits. Representative samples of what God desires for his people include living in or with peace, grace, freedom, hope, purity, holiness, renewed minds to approve God's will and being sanctified, rejoicing, praying, being thankful, obeying and doing good, and doing God's will—what God desires.

Unquestionably, the various writers view this calling (God's will) as central and normative: they extend this calling to the entire church that is in Christ. No Christian need wonder what our calling is. Calling identifies who we are and how we are to exhibit this identity. There is no mystery about it! All that remains is to decide whether to embrace the calling that the NT writers make abundantly clear we have in Christ. Peter exhorts, "Therefore, my brothers and sisters, make every effort to confirm your calling and election. For if you do these things, you will never stumble, and you will receive a rich welcome into the eternal kingdom of our Lord and Savior Jesus Christ" (2 Pet. 1:10–11). God calls his people to embrace the life God provided for them when he called and chose them. This is no mystery, not something that requires painstaking discovery. Read the Bible! Scripture makes clear what every believer's calling entails. The only question is whether we will "make every effort" to put this calling into practice in our lives.

Calling Taxonomy

In chapter 1 we introduced a taxonomy for categorizing recent writers on the topic of calling. Though a rough-and-ready schema, it provides a useful way of identifying the range of meaning for the term "calling" as it is used today. As we saw, some writers employ more than one of these meanings when they write about calling.

Categories of Calling

1. Calling is to a job, task, or role (whether secular or religious).
2. Calling is individualized and specific: what one is uniquely created to be or do.
3. Calling is dual/multiple: people have primary and secondary callings.
4. Calling is hidden and must be discovered through various means.
5. Calling is in Christ: believers find their calling in union with Christ and the church.

In our survey of writers since the early church, we saw where they fit into this suggested matrix of uses. In brief, the above list represents that taxonomy. Some authors' understanding of calling includes more than one of these categories. It is common to see calling explained as some combination of categories 1, 2, and 4. For such writers, God calls people to a specific job made precisely for them (1, 2). Often people must seek earnestly to discover that job (4), though for other writers, category 4 (the need for self-discovery) may be absent or more implicit than explicit. A subset of this group finds callings limited to *religious* vocations (1, 2, 4). Some writers see all jobs as callings, and whatever job one currently has (or might later pursue) is a valid calling (1). Usually, however, those adopting the view that all jobs are callings also affirm that Christians have a second calling—their calling as a Christian (5)—and thus Christians have two callings (3).

Others deny that calling is a job yet still believe that everyone has a unique "vocation" (2) that they must discover through various means (4). Indeed, it might take a person a long time—often through trial and error—to find their vocation, which exists for them irrespective of their job, if any.[4] Of course, a person might seek a job that enables them to fulfill their personal vocation (1, 2), though this may be impossible for many.

Finally, we found writers who limit their understanding of calling to the call to follow Christ (5). For them, calling becomes a matter of fulfilling the mandates of Christ's call on one's life, whatever one's job or circumstance might be.

Conclusions about Calling Language

While contemporary writers use calling language in all the five senses above, are they free simply to use words in any way they please? Are personal stories or anecdotes sufficient for explaining how God calls people? Can we use the special way God called Isaiah or Paul as a blueprint for how we should expect God's call to be manifested today? This raises the crucial question of normativity. Our survey of the biblical evidence shows how Christians today ought to understand the call of God on our lives. We firmly believe that understanding the Christian's calling as a "calling in Christ" (category 5) best matches how the biblical writers present the concept. God calls his people, the church, to embrace and exhibit in their lives certain behaviors and values, whatever their circumstances, whatever their job (indeed, whether or not they have a job), whatever their geographical location or time in history. God's "calling" is not hidden; the call is described plainly on the pages of the Bible, and each believer who is "in Christ" has been empowered by the Holy Spirit to fulfill that call. It is not specific to any individual; all Christians have the same calling to follow

4. David Brooks says, "The best advice I've heard for people in search of a vocation is to say yes to everything" (*Second Mountain*, 119).

Christ.[5] When we read in the Scriptures that God called prophets or apostles (or others) to serve him, we in no way challenge these findings. However, we have found that such examples are "special cases" and not meant to be normative and a paradigm for how God calls some or all Christians today.

What do we say, then, to those who use "calling" to refer to a job, whether secular or religious (category 1)? The Bible confirms that God called key leaders in the history of Israel and that Jesus appointed specific ones to be his apostles, but we have found no evidence that God calls others (much less all people) to specific jobs or roles. This amounts to taking the meaning of "call" in one use and applying it to another situation without warrant, like applying one meaning of "trunk" in the wrong context.

Likewise, we have found no evidence that a "call" from God marks specific individuals and enables them to perform roles for which God has uniquely designed them (2) or that they should diligently seek to discover this special role (4). Writers who use "calling" with this meaning believe that God has uniquely wired each person and that our task is to discover what we have been individually wired (called) to be or do, whether a writer, painter, musician, pastor, missionary, or something else. Although people may indeed be uniquely "wired" and although God does gift his people differently, no biblical evidence connects this with the concept of God's call.

God does distribute spiritual gifts to his people that uniquely qualify them for certain roles or tasks in the church, but we saw that this individual distribution of spiritual gifts is better understood as believers' "calling in Christ" (category 5). All Christians have spiritual gifts for building up the body of Christ (Eph. 4:12–13; 1 Pet. 4:10–11; 1 Cor. 12). Though one commonly hears of a "calling to teach," for example, it is more accurate to include

5. We stress that here we are describing "calling" as our calling in Christ. Certainly, the Holy Spirit has distributed different gifts to members of the body of Christ, gifts that may be specific to each individual.

teaching within the category of spiritual gifts. We have found no biblical evidence that God calls a specific teacher to some specific church or ministry venue.[6] "Bloom where you are planted"—not "find the location or task to which God has called you"—seems to best describe Paul's view of how Christians should live out their faith (see 1 Cor. 7:17–24). Using teaching as an example, it is certainly valid to infer that one must discover that gift, perhaps through trial and error. In this sense, then, we might say that a spiritual gift remains hidden (category 4) until one embraces it. But, we hasten to add, this pertains to discerning one's gifts, not one's "calling"; the NT does not label teaching as a calling.

Wanting it both ways (3), some writers grant that a Christian's fundamental calling is to be in Christ (5) but also insist on a secondary calling to a job or role, whether religious or secular (1), or a calling for which a person was uniquely created (2). But this becomes very confusing when presented to well-intentioned Christians and results in the many downsides we observed in chapter 1. It overlooks the rich biblical importance of Christians' "calling in Christ" and co-opts the label "calling" to elevate these other uses. And it risks diminishing or even neglecting our "calling in Christ" because these other uses—job, vocation—seem more urgent and tangible. As noted above, the biblical evidence best fits using "calling" to refer to our call to be a Christian (5). The other uses fail to have biblical support. There is only one way!

What about authors who insist on using meanings for "calling" that do not correspond to what we believe are the normative biblical uses? As we noted at the start of this chapter, every word has a semantic range (e.g., the range of meanings for "trunk"), and as we observed earlier from Lewis Carroll's *Through the Looking Glass*, people can use words to mean anything they want. Moreover, if they use them consistently and confidently enough

---

6. Apollos may seem to be an exception, but Scripture does not suggest that we should view his calling as normative.

(as many authors and speakers do), others will adopt these new meanings, not questioning whether they genuinely reflect how the Bible uses the term. But when this happens, we insist, much is lost. Chapter 1 captures some of the downsides of a confused understanding of calling. In addition, the "upside" of the Bible's robust usage of the word tends to be ignored or dismissed.

Now that we have compiled and assessed the biblical material, we need to use the data to help us construct a "theology of calling" for Christians to live by. For various reasons, theologies of calling have emerged and diverged over the centuries, and they exert enormous influence over people, especially for Christians who affirm that God is the agent of calling. In the next chapter, we will point the way to a theology of calling that incorporates the biblical data to fashion a way of living that truly honors the God who calls.

Uses of Calling Terminology in the Bible

By way of summary, we list here all the uses of calling language that we discovered in the Bible.

1. *God's appointment of "cultic" leaders in theocratic Israel* (e.g., patriarchs, Moses, kings, prophets, and priests). God called leaders to these specific "jobs" or ministries (whether political or religious) within national Israel. Individual Israelites were not called to specific jobs or roles (e.g., farmer, vinedresser, or carpenter) or to marry or remain single. These kinds of cultic "callings" were divine actions and normative only for Israel's leaders and not the general population.

2. *Israelites* (as individual members of the nation of Israel) *called to obedience, service, and witness.* The OT repeatedly stresses these values, so we should see them as normative for Israel. They are repeated and reinforced in the NT for Christians as members of the corporate Christ.

3. *Jesus's appointment of apostles, including Judas.* These are foundational tasks or roles in the establishment of the Jesus movement. Here we include Paul and other leaders foundational in establishing the church. They parallel the calling of national leaders in Israel. These foundational roles cannot be regarded as normative for how God chooses people for various jobs or occupations today, whether religious or secular.

4. *Jesus's commission of apostles to perform certain ministry tasks* (e.g., to preach, exorcise demons) *that are repeated as tasks for later followers of Jesus.* The tasks should be understood as normative for God's people if reinforced in the NT as ongoing and not limited to the position of an apostle. Yet various tasks may be limited by how they are employed in the Spirit's distribution of spiritual gifts. So while God may call Christians to preach or exorcise demons as general categories or tasks, they must discern how, in what circumstances, and whether they are gifted to do it. The "call" is to serve.

5. *The Holy Spirit's specific instructions to Paul about ministry locations* (though typically Paul moved to various locales on his own initiative). Specific, miraculous interventions were exceptions rather than the norm for those in ministry. The Spirit may of course give exceptional instructions to Jesus's servants as the Spirit wills.

6. *Believers called to salvation in Christ.* This is normative for today.

7. *The church is called "in Christ."* This is a corporate calling, establishing the *identity* of the church as the body of Christ, the saints or holy ones, God's people, those loved by God. This is by definition normative for God's people today.

8. *Believers share a calling to godly virtues and behaviors that determine the character of those in Christ.* This establishes the normative traits and functions of the church among its

members and in the world. It too is normative for God's people today.

9. *Offices and the requisite giftings for the functioning and building up of the church.* These are normative but, apart from the apostles, specific individuals are not generally "called" to fill these roles.

In summary, we conclude that the following are normative for Christians today (points 4 through 9 from the preceding list):

- *Jesus's commission of apostles to perform certain ministry tasks* (e.g., to preach, exorcise demons) *that are repeated as tasks for later followers of Jesus.* The tasks are reinforced beyond the Gospels and Acts as ongoing for Christ's followers and not limited to only the apostles.

- *The Holy Spirit's specific instructions to Paul about ministry locations* (though typically Paul moved to various locales on his own initiative). Though specific, miraculous interventions were exceptions rather than the norm, the Spirit may give exceptional instructions as the Spirit wills. Scripture gives no warrant for Christians today to solicit or expect such miraculous leadings.

- *Believers are called to salvation in Christ.* This constitutes the central invitation for sinners to enter into the body of Christ.

- *The church is called to be "in Christ."* This is a corporate calling, establishing the fundamental communal *identity* of the church: the body of Christ, the saints or holy ones, God's people, those loved by God. They are seated in the heavenly realms in Christ.

- *Believers share a calling to pursue godly virtues and behaviors that reflect the character of those in Christ.* This establishes the traits and functions of the church among its members and in the world.

- *Offices and the requisite giftings for the functioning and building up of the church.* Apart from the apostles, specific individuals are not generally "called" to fill these roles. That is, while not normative for Christians today, God may choose to call people in this way. Again, Scripture gives no warrant for Christians today to solicit or expect such miraculous leadings.

5

Constructing a Theological Map for Calling

Visiting and wandering around a new city can be quite an undertaking if you do not follow directions. Several years ago, one of us (Dan) learned this the hard way while visiting Washington, DC. My wife, Anna, our one-year-old firstborn, Josiah, and I visited a family member in Maryland. We decided to venture into Washington for a day to visit the sites. One of the places we wanted to visit was the US Bureau of Engraving and Printing, which did not offer reservations for tours but required arriving early in the morning to claim tickets on a first-come-first-served basis. We got up early one morning and took the Metro into the city. Our relative was quite familiar with the National Mall, instructing us to get off at the Smithsonian station, walk toward the Washington Monument, and turn left at the Holocaust Memorial Museum; our destination was just beyond that point. This seemed simple enough.

It just so happened, though, that I found a touristy map of the Mall while we rode the Metro. It was an illustrated map with colorful cartoon images of the major monuments and included the Metro lines and stations. Needless to say, the map was not to scale, nor was it complete in its depiction of every geographic feature along or near the National Mall. Its purpose was to give a general sense of where monuments were, probably serving better as a guide while walking the mall. As I looked at this map, I noticed that the L'Enfant Plaza station appeared to be closer to the Bureau of Engraving and Printing than the Smithsonian station was. Seeming brilliance struck me in that moment. I boldly declared to Anna a change of plans; my intuition told me we would save some time and energy by getting off at this "closer" station. And that is what we did. When we got off the train, we were like fish out of water. People wearing trench coats and carrying briefcases hurriedly walked in every direction around us. We stood on the platform as the only tourists in sight. Despite feeling a bit out of place, off we went.

We started walking in a direction that seemed right, based on the map I had found. Keep in mind that this was 2005; Siri provided no assistance. We found our way out of the station and onto a nearby street and could see no monuments. Yet this did not strike me as odd. We made our way along a nearby street in a direction I thought seemed right for our intended destination. Finally, after countless wrong turns, a frustrated wife, a crying baby, no Bureau of Engraving and Printing, and even a rainstorm, I decided to ask for directions. I still remember the look on the gentleman's face as he no doubt wondered how in the world we had ended up *there* as tourists. He gave us the directions we needed back to the Mall, and I followed them exactly. We finally found our destination, but we were wet and exhausted. To top it all off, no more visitor tickets were available for the Bureau of Engraving and Printing that day.

Intuition and arbitrary directional decision-making will get you somewhere, but if you want to end up in a particular location, it is wise to seek guidance from and trust a reliable source. In our survey of current, historical, and biblical uses of calling terminology we have seen that meanings and usages have evolved over time. In fact, they are all over the map! Mirroring our disastrous DC excursion, common usage of calling language has gone off-road, paving new trails and ending up in some questionable locations. This detour took centuries to develop, and finding the road again will not be easy, but this does not mean that we should not try to get back on course. If you discover that you are lost because you did not ask for directions (like you should have), the best thing to do is to retrace your steps, ask for help, and get back on track. We are not so far off the map that there is no hope for a clear passage to our desired destination: a correct understanding of calling. We do need some help, though, and a theological discussion with some reliable guides will point out some important landmarks that can help us along the way. We are not starting from scratch as we seek to devise a more adequate theological roadmap, one that gets us to the correct and biblical destination of calling as a way of life for all believers. In previous chapters we assessed the normative uses of calling terminology in the Bible along with the beliefs of key thinkers through the centuries. But as we will see, some theologians within the past century or so have found deficiencies in how many contemporary writers and speakers have understood calling (discussed in chap. 1). We believe they can offer us important insights as we navigate our way through this issue. We will see how they complement and reinforce the conclusions we came to in our biblical analyses. In many ways, we are not constructing a theology of calling from scratch but rather *re*constructing a theology of calling that underwent an unfortunate devolution over the past centuries.

To reconstruct a more useful theological roadmap in order to arrive at what we believe is the true biblical understanding of calling, we first need to deconstruct the current roadmaps and understand why they are inadequate. This will require discussion about the role experience plays in the development of theology and the need for theology to apply to all people in all circumstances. If our theology does not work for all people, especially at the margins of life, of what use is it? In chapter 1 we demonstrated the shadow side of calling's popular uses today by looking at several personal accounts.

Through the lens of theology we will address in this chapter some of the issues these popular uses raise. Because Martin Luther looms as such a key figure in the ongoing discussion about calling, we will consider Miroslav Volf's critique of Luther's view of work as vocation. We will then draw from the thinking of various theologians and propose three theological landmarks for our calling road map. These landmarks will be the basis for our own *klesiology*[1] and will provide direction and clarity regarding who we are as God's people (our identity) and how we are to live in the world (our mission).

Faith Seeking Understanding (in the Real World)

Anselm of Canterbury famously described the task of theology as *fides quaerens intellectum* (faith seeking understanding). For Anselm, faith and understanding were inseparable: "For I do not seek to understand so that I may believe, but I believe so that I may understand."[2] Though he may have coined this oft-quoted phrase, Anselm was not the originator of the idea. Before him, Augustine observed, "I believe in order that I may understand."[3] Before Augustine, Jesus affirmed Thomas despite his doubts (John 20:24–29) and showed that it is okay not to have all the answers at a given moment. Over two thousand years later, theologians agree that "faith and inquiry are inseparable."[4] But understanding is more than mere cognitive assent to some abstract principles. Our functional epistemologies engage real time and space. In other words, our understanding happens in the real world, with all its limitations, frustrations, and brokenness. Therefore, the understanding and expression of our faith must be meaningful and functional amid the varied and often trying circumstances in which God's people find themselves.

1. Kuzmič, *"Beruf and Berufung."* On the basis of the Greek noun *klēsis* (call), Kuzmič uses the term "klesiology" as shorthand for his constructed theology of calling. We use the same term here as shorthand for our own constructed theology of calling.
2. Anselm, *Anselm of Canterbury*, 87.
3. Augustine, *Confessions and Enchiridion*, 338.
4. Migliore, *Faith Seeking Understanding*, 1.

Beth Felker Jones observes that "Christian theology is a conversation about Scripture, about how to read and interpret it better, how to understand the Bible as a whole and imagine a way of life that is faithful to the God whose Word this is."[5] This sort of theological imagination does not conceive make-believe worlds such as Narnia or Middle Earth. Rather, it considers what it means to appropriate the truths of Scripture, written two millennia ago, within the varied, changing, and often complex particularities of our own circumstances today. A translation is needed, not from Greek or Hebrew into English, but from biblical particularities into contemporary particularities; from a written source that is fixed and unchanging to a myriad of real-life contexts that are constantly in flux.[6] This is why theological reflection must take place in every generation.[7] We need to continue imagining faithful ways forward amid circumstances we have never encountered before, such as a global pandemic (in which we find ourselves as we write these words).

Applying our theological imaginations to the topic of calling is far more than a semantic battle. It is about giving freedom and providing a pathway for unity to God's people in Christ in the real-world circumstances where they find themselves. It concerns the Christian hope that all God's people will flourish as they are faithful to their calling in Christ and experience "life . . . to the full" (John 10:10) as Jesus promised. And it is about strengthening the gospel witness of the church in the world. Charles Taylor coined the phrase "modern social imaginaries."[8] Taylor had in mind "the ways in which [people] imagine their social existence, how they fit together with others, how things go on between them

---

5. Jones, *Practicing Christian Doctrine*, 2.
6. See Lee, "Reading Scripture in Our Context."
7. Our current theological reflections are challenging contemporary understandings of calling and paving a redirected and newly imagined way forward based on sound biblical exegesis. As theological reflection takes place in every generation, it must address contemporary challenges *and* reflect sound biblical exegesis.
8. Taylor, *Secular Age*, 159–218.

and their fellows, the expectations which are normally met, and the deeper normative notions and images which underlie these expectations."[9] These imaginaries are not grounded in arbitrary ideals of goodness but rather are anchored in the gospel. Taylor continues, "The Gospel generates the idea of a community of saints, inspired by love for God, for each other, and for human-kind, whose members were devoid of rivalry, mutual resentment, love of gain, ambition to rule, and the like."[10] A reconstructed theological imagination of calling must extend well beyond indi-vidually pursuing fulfillment in one's work, ministry, or personal passion. Such a selfish reduction cuts faithfulness off at the knees and not only ignores what the gospel of Jesus Christ entails but also misses a powerful opportunity to bring freedom and unity to God's people through the gospel.

We do not want to jump too far ahead of ourselves, though. We must first trudge through some arduous terrain, if we hope to get back on track; we need to realize how lost we are and how we got off the path. If theology is "faith seeking understanding," and if this understanding is anchored in the real world, we must take an honest and realistic look at people's lived realities in this world. We need to enter other people's experiences.[11] To help us understand why we need a reconstructed klesiology (as we sug-gested in chap. 2), we will first interact with Miroslav Volf. He will help deconstruct our popular understanding of calling, which all too often conflates calling with work or a job.

A Practical Deconstruction of Popular Notions of Calling

In chapter 1, we viewed several examples of the shadow side to the popular use of calling terminology today. We related personal

9. Taylor, *Secular Age*, 171.
10. Taylor, *Secular Age*, 161.
11. For a deeper theological dive entering the experiences of others, see Williams, *Bonhoeffer's Black Jesus*.

accounts of how the unintended side effects of particular uses of calling terminology left people frustrated, confused, disappointed, and hurt—hardly the sort of life that God intends for us to experience in Christ. These personal accounts reflect genuine inadequacies in how calling language is being used. An adequate theology of calling must address these faults and help God's people live faithfully within their varied circumstances; it must not be simply a theology of the moment, like a current fad. We acknowledge that theologians develop (imagine) theology within their own contexts and that it can be difficult to recognize one's own limited perspective. These limitations invariably hinder theologians' ability to address future realities and might cause later readers to regard earlier theological thinking as condescending at worst or irrelevant at best.[12] Such is the case as we consider Martin Luther's sixteenth-century thinking about vocation in light of our own circumstances today. Luther's theology reflects his attempt to come to terms with his own world, and in the process, he came to some conclusions that we consider misguided.

Luther did not set out to develop a theology of calling. Rather, as other aspects of his theology developed, so too did his theology of calling and work—or as it is often described, his theology of vocation.[13] Miroslav Volf observes that justification by faith was Luther's basis for his understanding of vocation, and one of his "most culturally influential accomplishments was to overcome the monastic reduction of *vocatio* to a calling to a particular kind of religious life."[14] Despite the importance of Luther's thinking on this matter, and the valuable role it played in ushering in the Protestant Reformation, his theology developed within a particular

12. Although we as authors are doing the best we can, we are unaware of possible blind spots; this is why our thinking must be seen as just another contribution among others in an ongoing theological conversation.

13. For a full treatment of Luther's doctrine of vocation, see Wingren, *Luther on Vocation.*

14. Volf, *Work in the Spirit,* 105.

time and set of circumstances and was based on his interpretation of specific Bible passages.

Among the biblical texts Luther used to develop his theology of vocation, 1 Cor. 7 was primary. His interpretation of this passage, though, has been questioned.[15] While his understanding of *vocatio* did indeed bring about a broader understanding of what constituted sacred work, it also led to our popular reduction of calling to one's gainful employment. As a result of his exegesis and application, "Luther starts later Christians down the path of thinking that everyone had a *Beruf*—a station, social role, estate, or occupation that gave one a holy calling from God."[16] Luther's application of *vocatio*—in particular, that a person remains in a "calling" (i.e., blacksmith, farmer, etc.) for one's whole life— underscores the importance of undergirding any real-world application with sound biblical exegesis. Faulty exegesis leads to unhelpful applications of calling. This is why our interaction with the thought of Miroslav Volf has proved crucial to our own theological reflections on calling.

In his book *Work in the Spirit*, Volf affirms Luther's important contributions to our understanding of work but also describes six limitations of Luther's theology of vocation.[17] These limitations are more than merely abstract observations: they show an incongruence between Luther's exegesis and subsequent theology of vocation and many people's lived experiences today.

1. Volf first mentions how equating vocation with work can lead to an indifference toward alienation in work.[18] Luther believed that God ordained people to live and work within particular stations in life. If a person was born into a family of blacksmiths, this was ordained by God. Blacksmith work was considered to be

---

15. Volf's critique, which we are exploring in depth, is one of the most extensive critiques. See also Bonhoeffer, *Ethics*, 289; Waalkes, "Rethinking Work as Vocation."

16. Waalkes, "Rethinking Work as Vocation," 139.

17. Volf's book was first published in 1991, but the same general challenges still apply. We have simply provided contemporary examples to illustrate his points.

18. Volf, *Work in the Spirit*, 107.

the vocation of the family members because it was God's calling for them to work in that particular station, and their work was rendered as service to others. As a result, individuals called to specific stations in life must stay within that station, regardless of their circumstances. While Luther's affirmation of all types of work is commendable, Volf recognizes that not all types of work do indeed dignify the worker: "If even the 'lifting of a single straw' is a 'completely divine work,' there is no reason why the same description could not apply to the most degrading types of work in industrial and information societies."[19]

For those who have the opportunity to pursue desirable or noble work rather than oppressive and dehumanizing work, conflating work and calling is a privilege; but this conflation is not consistent with the experiences of many. Take, for example, the conditions many endure while working for large retail companies that pursue profit at the expense of employees.[20] If we are to be consistent in devising a theology of calling that applies to all people, we must do so in a way that upholds workers' dignity, regardless of their circumstances and the nature of their work. Has God called people to work in oppressive work environments, or has he called them to discern how to faithfully live out their calling to Christ amid difficult and oppressive work environments? We must not allow our theological conclusions to legitimize oppressive cultural and industry practices at the expense of the dignity and health of the worker. But these are some of the unintended consequences of Luther's view.

2. Volf also points us toward a dangerous ambiguity in Luther's conception of vocation. For Luther, the believer experiences both a spiritual and an external calling—a spiritual calling that comes through the proclamation of the gospel, and an external calling

19. Volf, *Work in the Spirit*, 107. Volf cites Luther, *WA* 10/I.1:317.
20. For example, consider the reported working conditions of Amazon employees: Taddonio, "'You're Just Disposable'"; Hamilton and Cain, "Amazon Warehouse Employees Speak Out."

that comes through one's specific station in life. Functionally, it is far too easy for the external calling to carry more weight and importance than the spiritual calling so that one's vocation as work becomes the primary focus. As we observed in chapter 1, this very dynamic has taken root in a popular understanding of calling today, exemplified in Os Guinness speaking of a primary and secondary calling.

Presumably, the terms "primary" and "secondary" calling are intended to communicate that a person's salvation in Christ holds primary significance and that any other particular type of life calling is subordinate to it. Yet in dominant popular usage, the primary way Christians talk about their calling is in individualistic terms related to a particular job, task, or ministry. The same ambiguity in Luther's thinking about vocation needs clarification. We believe clarity will come when we stop distinguishing between spiritual and external or primary and secondary as it relates to the Christian's calling. This clarity will help Christians see that there is not a calling hierarchy. Instead, their calling is to Christ, and the subsequent manner in which they are to live their life (in holiness) applies to every domain of their life—not just their job.[21]

3. There is a danger when we ideologically equate work with one's calling. Here Volf brings together the first two limitations he sees in Luther's theology of vocation, observing that a "problem arises when one combines such a high valuation of work with both indifference to alienation and the identification of calling with occupation."[22] Volf speaks of people who work in dehumanizing conditions or, as he puts it, whose work is reduced to "soulless movement."[23] There is often a great chasm between ideology and reality. When one's work reality is fraught with the effects of the fall and the reality of finitude, the idea that everyone has a special

---

21. This reminds us of Jesus's answer when questioned about paying taxes to Caesar (Mark 12:13–17). God does not demand part or most of his people's loyalty: he requires all of it.
22. Volf, *Work in the Spirit*, 108.
23. Volf, *Work in the Spirit*, 108.

job, task, or ministry that they were made for (a "calling") seems fanciful and insufficient. We must be careful not to romanticize calling in a way that elevates the work of some and patronizes those enduring hard and inhumane work experiences. This flaw can also blind us to the need to address systemic issues that lead to these dehumanizing work experiences. Expanding our understanding of calling beyond an individualized prompting toward personal fulfillment requires us to pursue the flourishing of all those in Christ.

4. Volf observes that "calling" as a job or vocation is simply "not applicable to the increasingly mobile industrial and information society."[24] Gone are the days when most people worked a single job or worked for a single company for their entire career.[25] What happens to the notion of "calling to a job" when these transitions happen more frequently? As technology increases, robots take over some people's jobs. Take the trucking industry, for example.[26] In an industry known for harsh work environments, automation projections point us toward a future where big-rig trucks will be self-propelled and driverless. What will happen to those whose careers have been defined by this one kind of work? While there will be opportunity for some to pivot into more technology-driven roles within the industry, will there be room for all? In any case, how does one apply calling-as-work to this sort of situation? If God calls people to particular lines of work, and entire industries are upended or eliminated due to technological advances, what happens to God's calling when people's jobs go away?

As we write this, the world is reeling from the COVID-19 pandemic. Unemployment has soared to new heights, and what were once considered "givens" regarding job security have gone away.[27] The food and travel industries have been hit extremely hard.

---

24. Volf, *Work in the Spirit*, 108.
25. U.S. Bureau of Labor Statistics, "National Longitudinal Surveys."
26. Semuels, "When Robots Take Bad Jobs."
27. M. Klein, "Coronavirus Hasn't Spared White Collar Jobs"; Feintzeig, "Do You Dare Switch Jobs?"

Adaptation and change are the new norms, whether for those who are looking for new types of work or for those who must learn to do their work in a new way. As life returns to "normal," much confusion abounds about what that should look like. Should vaccinations be required for employees? Should employees be forced to return to their offices? Educators accustomed to teaching within classrooms had to adjust to teaching online. Both now and in the future, the level of work adaptation—whether driven by a virus or massive societal changes—necessitates reimagining our understanding and theology of calling. If theology is "faith seeking understanding" in the real world, these changing realities must play a more significant role in our understanding of calling. This does not mean that as occupational circumstances change, so too must one's calling change: from this calling, to that, then to none, then to still another. Rather, we contend that the Christian's calling in Christ *does not change* even when circumstances (or jobs) change. Therefore, Christians' calling to live a holy life in Christ applies in any new or adjusted circumstance in which they find themselves.

5. Many people today experience what Volf calls a "synchronic plurality of employments or jobs."[28] Many people must work multiple jobs to survive and make ends meet. Many factors contribute to this. For example, the cost of living continues to increase in many cities while wages do not rise proportionally. Lesser-skilled jobs simply do not provide enough income for families to survive. Many young people graduate from college owing thousands of dollars in school debt, and an entry-level full-time job is not enough to support them as they pay down their loans. A gig economy is an increasing reality for many workers, leaving them without income when between jobs and with little or no health insurance. We could go on. For the foreseeable future, there will likely be even more reasons for people to work multiple jobs.

28. Volf, *Work in the Spirit*, 109.

If someone works multiple jobs, to which of those jobs, if any, are they called? What happens when someone drops or adds a job to their assortment of occupations? Do they lose and gain callings at the whim of economic circumstances? Our current work landscape provides a significant reason why a reconstructed theology of calling is needed. There is one calling for the Christian *in Christ*. The Christian does not need to update their calling portfolio as life circumstances change or new opportunities arise. Instead, they simply need to discern the shape of faithfulness and holiness in whatever circumstance they find themselves.

6. Finally, Volf reveals an easily overlooked challenge when we reduce calling to gainful employment. He writes, "The reduction of vocation to employment, coupled with the belief that vocation is the primary service ordinary people render to God, contributed to the modern fateful elevation of work to the status of religion."[29] In this way, when equated with calling, work has become an idol for too many people. Perhaps this is a reason why, according to a Gallup poll, majorities of workers consistently say they find their identity in their work.[30] Pew Research Center conducted a similar study, and found that the more education persons have, the more likely they are to gain their sense of identity from their work. In their finding, 38 percent of those with only a high school degree found their identity in their work, while 77 percent of those with a postgraduate degree found their identity in their work.[31] Finding significance in one's work is desirable and commendable when possible. However, conflating one's work with one's calling is quite problematic and runs the risk of turning work into an idol and thus an identity-forming reality. We are not what we do! Anchoring our calling in Christ is meant to shape our identity rather than the work that is in front of us.

29. Volf, *Work in the Spirit*, 109.
30. Riffkin, "In U.S., 55% of Workers Get Sense of Identity from Their Job."
31. Pew Research Center, "State of American Jobs."

Volf is not alone in critiquing modern notions of calling and vocation.[32] Lori Brandt Hale explores the topic by interacting with Dietrich Bonhoeffer's christological take on vocation. She observes that Bonhoeffer "provides a way to understand vocation as a hermeneutic or interpretive lens that shapes and orients one's way of living in the world and in relationship to that world, to God and to others."[33] We need to do more than critique unhelpful notions of calling, though. Like Hale, we believe a vigorous theology of calling will reorient God's people toward a different way of viewing God and themselves and engaging others and the surrounding world. More specifically, a reoriented theology of calling will lead God's people to see their calling in terms of who they are in Christ, locating their calling corporately rather than individually. Then they can see the whole of their lives not merely as a series of tasks but as the arena for working out their calling as an identity. At this point we are poised to construct our reoriented theology of calling, our klesiology, which will build on and provide adequate responses to Volf's critique of Luther's understanding of work as vocation. In what follows, we engage as conversation partners Dietrich Bonhoeffer, Karl Barth, Lesslie Newbigin, and Ray Anderson—but we begin with the theme of being called in Christ.

A Theological Reorientation of Calling

Calling and Christ

As we engage in theological reflection on calling and thus develop a reoriented klesiology, we believe that a theology worthy of the name must be rooted in Scripture. It will help to begin by considering some of the shortest and perhaps most overlooked words within our English language: prepositions have tremendous

---

32. See, e.g., Hale, "Bonhoeffer's Christological Take on Vocation"; Waalkes, "Rethinking Work as Vocation."

33. Hale, "Bonhoeffer's Christological Take on Vocation," 176.

theological import. Prepositions describe relationships between objects: I walk *around* the pond; the dog is *under* the table; the airplane flew *over* the ocean. We use them all the time in conversation with others. Their very existence in our language reminds us of the relational nature of life. We can never rid our language of prepositions, because we cannot rid ourselves of relating to the world and others around us. We also use prepositions to describe our relationship with God: I pray *to* God; the Holy Spirit is present *with* us; I am *in* Christ. These prepositions indicate a participatory aspect to our relationship with the Triune God.[34] These same prepositions play an important theological role in the NT as Paul, John, and Peter use them to describe various aspects of our relationship with God.

When reading the NT and specifically some of the key passages on calling, we find a strong prepositional theology related to who we are *in* Christ. In chapter 3 we looked at several passages, especially in the Epistles, that describe the normative uses of calling language—language that applies to all believers at all times in all cultures and circumstances.[35] Incorporation into or union with Christ stands out.[36]

> Christians are called "*into* fellowship with [the] Son," and because of God we are "*in* Christ Jesus" (1 Cor. 1:9, 30).
>
> God has called us to live "*in* the grace of Christ" (Gal. 1:6).
>
> We are called to a holy life because of the "grace . . . given us *in* Christ Jesus" (2 Tim. 1:9).
>
> God has called us by "his . . . glory and goodness" so that we "might participate *in* the divine nature" (2 Pet. 1:3–4).[37]

34. See Vanhoozer's "From 'Blessed in Christ' to 'Being in Christ'"; on p. 13 he discusses the reality of "prepositional theology."

35. We review several passages already explored in chap. 3 to reinforce the biblical basis for identifying these as theological landmarks.

36. For a more comprehensive study, see Campbell, *Paul and Union with Christ*.

37. Emphasis added in all these quotations.

The Christian's calling is about who we are in Christ. It is not about the particularities of our life circumstances, such as our occupation, where we live, what we feel wired to do, or to whom we are related.

In light of the modern-day emphasis on calling as an individualized and self-discovered job, task, or ministry, we need to grasp the implications of our participation in and with Christ. This participation in and with Christ is not merely our primary calling; it *is* our calling. We next highlight again two passages in Paul's Letters that demonstrate an important connection between the calling we have in Christ and the implications of living out that calling in the real world.

1 Corinthians 1

The Corinthian church was not a model of unity and faithfulness, to say the least. In his first letter to them, Paul writes to address several dysfunctions and unfaithful realities plaguing this congregation. However, Paul does not start his letter by bringing up their dysfunctions and shortcomings. Rather, he begins by reminding the Corinthians of who they are in Christ, and he does so by pointing them to their calling. In 1 Cor. 1:1 he starts by identifying himself with them as those called by God. For Paul, an application of his calling was his role as an apostle. The Corinthians did not have the same appointment to apostleship, but God called them to be "holy people" (1:2). This is not merely about living a moral life; rather, holiness is the intended result of their calling to fellowship with Jesus (1:9). Their calling is not arbitrary or a treasure to be discovered but rather extends to all the Corinthian believers, "both Jews and Greeks" (1:24). This calling is not to a particular job, task, or role but constitutes their union with Christ. Paul wants them to remember who they were when God called them in Christ (1:26). Simply trying harder will not lead to the sort of unity God intends and Paul desires for the Corinthians. The church will only experience unity when it embraces its calling to Christ and the implications of this calling for its identity and the corporate life that follows. A dysfunctional, divided, and disobedient church needs to be reminded of their identity as those called to and in Christ. Any other starting point is inadequate.

Ephesians 4

Paul uses the first half of the Letter to the Ephesians to line out the blessings of being chosen by God and what it means to be in Christ.[38] He pivots in chapter 4 to discuss practical matters of how this looks in the readers' day-to-day lives. Paul urges them "to live a life worthy of the calling you have received" (Eph. 4:1; see also 2 Thess. 1:11).[39] This calling is the calling to Christ, to participate in the life of the Son. As Christians live their lives, they are to do so in a manner that is worthy of this calling. The Greek term for "worthy," *axios*, indicates a scale used to determine the relative value of two objects.[40] Christians should live lives that measure up to their calling in Christ. In Eph. 4:2–3 Paul identifies humility, gentleness, patience, tolerance, love, unity, and peace as marks of the lives that are worthy of Christ's calling. For Paul, calling describes the way the Ephesians live in the whole of their lives. These qualities overlap with what Paul tells the Corinthians. The life of holiness that the church is called to embrace finds expression in these Spirit-generated qualities, all enabled because they are in Christ. Faithfully living out this calling results in unity in the church (Eph. 4:3–6). Calling denotes the church's identity in Christ and, correspondingly, the sort of life God desires for those who participate in the life of Christ.

38. E.g., see Paul's uses of "in Christ" in Eph. 1:3–4, 6–7, 9, 11; 2:5–6, 10, 21–22; 3:6, 11–12.

39. In a parallel way, Paul urges the Philippians to live lives that are "worthy of the gospel" (Phil. 1:27).

40. *EDNT*, "Ἄξιος," 1:113; cf. BDAG, "Ἄξιος," 93–94; *NIDNTTE*, "Ἄξιος," 1:340–42.

Participation in Christ is a dominant theme in Paul's Letters.[41] It is also the substance of Dietrich Bonhoeffer's theological reflections on calling and vocation. He writes, "In encounter with Jesus Christ, a person experiences God's call [*Ruf*], and in it the calling [*Berufung*] to a life in community with Jesus Christ."[42] For Bonhoeffer, calling was not about a specific job, task, or vocation but rather about living life in community with Christ and others. Calling is not specific to a particular circumstance of one's life but extends to the whole of life, which is marked by living in community with Christ. As a result, there is no limit to the ways in which Christians might faithfully express their calling in Christ. Bonhoeffer is especially concerned with the concrete expression of one's calling through *responsibility*. He writes, "From Christ's perspective this life is now my vocation; from my own perspective it is my responsibility."[43] A Christian's entire life constitutes the believer's calling, not merely some piece or part of it. Calling to Christ becomes a rubric of sorts that helps Christians determine what a faithful and responsible action might be amid whatever circumstances they find themselves. This sounds much like Paul's exhortation to the Ephesians: "Walk [in a manner] worthy of the calling you have received" (Eph. 4:1 CSB).

This point argues against any attempt to equate calling with a particularity in life, such as a job. In Bonhoeffer's mind, this is actually irresponsible. He insists, "Vocation is responsibility, and responsibility is the whole response of the whole person to reality as a whole. This is precisely why a myopic self-limitation to one's vocational obligations in the narrowest sense [such as a job or ministry] is out of the question; such a limitation would be

41. For further study on the topic of participation in Christ, see Campbell, *Paul and Union with Christ*; Gorman, *Becoming the Gospel*; Gorman, *Participating in Christ*; Macaskill, *Living in Union with Christ*; Thate, Vanhoozer, and Campbell, *"In Christ" in Paul*.
42. Bonhoeffer, *Ethics*, 290.
43. Bonhoeffer, *Ethics*, 290.

irresponsibility."[44] If persons are in Christ, their calling to Christ extends to the whole of their lives. Saying that one is called to be a pastor or called to be a doctor wrongly restricts the scope of one's responsibility to live faithfully as one who is in Christ. Instead, the whole of one's life, composed of all the particularities of their situation and circumstances at any given moment, defines and limits the scope of their responsibility to live faithfully in Christ. Extending calling to the whole of one's life means no circumstance or situation of life is outside the scope of a Christian's calling. All of life is a calling in Christ.

Karl Barth affirms Bonhoeffer's thinking about vocation, in particular reinforcing that vocation is "the place of responsibility."[45] He frames responsibility, though, in terms of obedience— obedience first to Christ's call and, second, obedience within one's particular life circumstances. As "calling" relates to one's responsibility to live a life of obedience, Barth recognizes that there is freedom in Christ for the Christian, but this freedom has limitations. These limitations provide the framework for Christians to express their calling to Christ. First, Barth identifies a person's *age* as a limiting factor. Each person experiences "gradually changing conditions of [their] psychophysical existence."[46] As people called to Christ mature from childhood to adolescence to adulthood, they have different sorts of responsibilities and opportunities to live a life of obedience. The energy that one has in one's twenties and thirties to be a youth pastor who plans and leads retreats and all-nighters is not the same level of energy one has in one's forties and fifties. By no means does this exclude those who are further along in life from engaging in youth ministry, but one's age and stage of life limits what one can do and sometimes what one even wants to do. In this example, one's calling does

---

44. Bonhoeffer, *Ethics*, 293.
45. Barth, *Church Dogmatics*, III/4:264. The subsection that deals with calling and vocation in Bonhoeffer, *Ethics*, is titled "The Place of Responsibility."
46. Barth, *Church Dogmatics*, III/4:274.

not change because one's energy level or desire to be a youth pastor diminishes. Rather, one's calling to Christ remains intact no matter one's age, though the shape of one's obedience as one who is in Christ adjusts.

Second, Barth observes that the *historical situation* limits how believers express their calling in Christ. Included in a historical situation are one's "country, century, generation and ancestry, the comprehensive state of political, economic, cultural and ecclesiastical affairs, the nature and level of humanity, habits, intellectual conceptions and morality in . . . [the] immediate environment."[47] Often one cannot choose such elements of one's broader context and environment. We as authors were born in the United States in the twentieth century. We were not born in Armenia in the fifth century. Christians living in Armenia at that time contended with many realities almost completely foreign to us—including their understanding of how to express their Christian faith. And vice versa, our Armenian sisters and brothers of the fifth century could never imagine the shape and texture of life and Christian faithfulness in the twenty-first century, let alone in a country that was unknown to them in their time. The various factors of our historical situation not only shape who we are but also determine the limits within which we strive to live in obedience in Christ. This second limitation resides outside the person. Again, Barth believes that one's calling cannot be understood apart from acknowledging these kinds of limitations.

Barth's third limitation resides within the person: one's *personal aptitude*.[48] Each person has certain skills, abilities, and inclinations. There is a level of usefulness each person offers based on what they have the capacity to do. Speaking personally, our skills, abilities, and inclinations have led us to work in the world of academia and coaching—teaching, researching, mentoring,

---

47. Barth, *Church Dogmatics*, III/4:284–85.
48. Barth, *Church Dogmatics*, III/4:289.

and writing books such as this one. Not every person has this same skill set and should therefore not be expected to express their obedience in this same way. Others are able to design propulsion systems for underwater vessels; we do not possess those skills. But neither "seminary professor" nor "engineer" are callings. We have seen seminary students claim to have a calling to be a pastor and yet not have the competency to preach, sit with people empathetically, or lead a group of people. Rather than conflate calling with a job, Barth reminds us that it is wise for Christians to embrace their calling to Christ and discern how to express this calling in and through the various abilities and skills they have.

Barth's final limitation is *obedience* in the Christian's particular "sphere of operation, the field of . . . ordinary everyday activity."[49] This limitation is similar to the second one mentioned above; yet here the emphasis lies not on the contextual elements of one's life but on one's obedience extending to the whole of life. Calling is not limited to one's gainful employment: "That a man's vocation [calling] is exhausted in his profession is no more true than that God's calling which comes to him is simply an impulsion to work. He will always live in widely different spheres if he receives the divine calling and is obedient to it."[50] While there is a tendency to myopically identify a specific aspect of our lives with our calling, Barth helps us lift our eyes to see that the whole of our lives is like a canvas on which an artist chooses to paint. No part of the canvas is off-limits, but the canvas has edges, and the artist should not go beyond these boundaries and paint the nearby dog or table. There is ultimately freedom for Christians to explore the shape of their obedience in Christ as they live within their varied spheres. In this way, Christians have

49. Barth, *Church Dogmatics*, III/4:296.
50. Barth, *Church Dogmatics*, III/4:265. "Man" is used generically here to include everyone.

the freedom to engage all aspects of their lives in ways that are worthy of their calling in Christ.

At the intersection of responsibility and limitation, those who are in Christ must discern how to live their lives in a manner that reflects that they participate in Christ. This means that participating in Christ concerns who they are in the whole of their lives rather than what they do in a particular job, task, or role. That Christians participate in Christ must occupy the most prominent place in their understanding of who they are and therefore how they live in the whole of their lives. Rather than identify a particular job, task, or role with one's calling, Christians must start with and subsequently emphasize what it means to live a life worthy of participating in the one to whom they are called and affirm their identity as God's people. Being in Christ is not just an individual reality, though. The individual focus of the dominant contemporary uses of calling language often leads us to overlook an important connection between the individual and the community. We turn our attention now to the topic of how the Christian's calling in Christ relates to the corporate body of Christ.

Calling's Corporate Nature

By default, Western readers filter *calling* through an individualistic lens; indeed, that is how we might be tempted to read Bonhoeffer and Barth's reflections. As we saw, Paul's uses of calling language in 1 Cor. 1 and Eph. 4 were corporate, referring to the church as a body. Paul uses plural pronouns that we may misread as singular. "Walk in a manner worthy of the calling you have" could be more accurately translated as "Conduct your lives in a manner worthy of the calling with which you *all* were called *together*."[51] On many topics (esp. relating to the topic of calling) our tendency is first to consider the implications for *me* and then move to *we*. Paul starts with *we*, and then the readers are left to

---

51. Eph. 4:1, our trans.

consider what it means for *me*. This starting point and subsequent directional move are significant.

In his reflections on the nature of the church, Lesslie Newbigin affirms this corporate reality. He observes, "Every Christian has his life in Christ only as a member in the body of Christ. He shares in the life of Christ only by sharing it with all His people. The new birth, the new man in Christ, is a social reality."[52] Not only does this statement emphasize the corporate nature of the church; it is also substantiated by the same "in Christ" theology we discussed above. Newbigin's ecclesiological reflections start with Abraham, who "was called out from his land and people to become the father of the faithful, by whom the apostles themselves were chosen to be witnesses of Christ."[53] While some point to Abraham's calling as an example of how God "calls" individuals to specific jobs, tasks, or roles (as we noted in chap. 3), it is more important to assert that Abraham's story constitutes the appointment of one man through whom a nation would be called to become God's people (Gen. 12:2–3). God called Abraham to father a nation, a nation that would eventually bring forth the Messiah (Rom. 9:5), in whom *we* are now called to be God's people (4:11–12; 9:24–26).[54] Just as there was a new people (Israel) brought into existence through one man, Abraham, so too is there in Christ "a new creation, a new humanity."[55]

This corporate calling entails a crucial functional element. As an essential component of God's redemptive work in the world, the church's calling is to be "the extension of His saving power to the whole world."[56] How is this saving power made manifest

52. Newbigin, *Household of God*, 118. We have retained Newbigin's wording, although he doubtless intends the masculine pronouns to be understood generically.

53. Newbigin, *Household of God*, 33.

54. See our discussion of the nation Israel's call under "Corporate Calling," in chap. 3.

55. Newbigin, *Household of God*, 36. Paul employs this same construct of corporate solidarity when he contrasts humanity "in Adam" with those "in Christ" (Rom. 5:12–21; 1 Cor. 15:22).

56. Newbigin, *Household of God*, 52.

in the world? It is not through accurate doctrinal statements and creedal affirmations alone. In fact, Newbigin criticizes the Western church for being overly intellectual and believing that church unity is found through the "teaching and acceptance of correct doctrine."[57] Newbigin makes an important point that an overemphasis on internal congregational doctrinal agreement has led to the "virtual disappearance of the idea of the church as a visible unity."[58] For Newbigin, the Christian calling is corporate and leads to the sending of God's people into the world as the priesthood of all believers.[59] This is the work of the church: when a church gathers, it should equip and empower God's called people to go forth into the world. The church's collective calling is the same—to Christ—but this calling manifests itself through an infinite number of expressions in the world.

Ray Anderson provides some complementary reflections on calling that expand on Newbigin's thoughts. Anderson anchors calling not in a mystical experience of revelation that there is a particular job, task, or role in which one must participate, but rather in baptism: "There is a sense in which one can say that baptism into Christ is ordination into the ministry of Christ. As Christ was called and ordained to His Messianic ministry through baptism, so the baptism of every person can be viewed as a calling into the ministry of Christ. The special ordination that sets baptized persons apart as representative of the ministry of Christ through the church is still grounded upon baptism."[60]

For Anderson, baptism is more than an individual's public declaration of personal faith. He asserts, "Whatever theological connotations baptism may have as a ritual of the church, for the

---

57. Newbigin, *Household of God*, 53.
58. Newbigin, *Household of God*, 54.
59. For more on this see Newbigin, *Truth to Tell*, esp. chap. 3. The priesthood of all believers means not that all believers are priests in the formal sense but rather that all believers are ministers, serving Christ in their public lives. On the priest theme found throughout Scripture, see Beale, *The Temple and the Church's Mission*.
60. Anderson, *Soul of Ministry*, 84.

individual it can have great significance as a reinforcement of authentic personhood."[61] The sense of personhood experienced in baptism is not about one's individualism; instead, it is located in the context of the community of believers. Anderson observes that baptism is a liturgical function, but he defines liturgy as "a particular offering to God of that which is appropriate to him," or simply, "one who serves."[62] A liturgy is not merely an expression of worship within a church service but consists of the service the people themselves offer both inside and outside a local church gathering.[63]

However, Anderson understands liturgy as much more than an individual's experience. Rather than viewing liturgy through an individualistic lens, he instead posits: "The fundamental liturgical paradigm of personhood is community."[64] He explains: "The liturgical events which are intrinsic to community are rituals of reinforcement for human personhood. Community is more than a social event, it is the re-enactment of the personhood of Christ himself (his body), and the manifestation of his own service. This ongoing ministry of Christ through his humanity continues through the human community as his body."[65]

In this line of thinking, the individual identifies with Christ through baptism, but the event of baptism also identifies the individual as a member of the corporate body of believers (1 Cor. 12:13). As a part of the corporate body of believers (those who are together called to Christ), individual Christians must *then* discern the shape of their ministry. This ministry is indeed not limited to formal activities of the local church, nor is it monopolized by those who receive their paychecks by engaging in "full-time ministry." Rather, as Newbigin affirms above, this ministry extends beyond the private and into the public spaces

61. Anderson, *On Being Human*, 179.
62. Anderson, *On Being Human*, 180.
63. For more on this point, see W. Klein, "Can You Worship Anyplace?"
64. Anderson, *On Being Human*, 182.
65. Anderson, *On Being Human*, 183.

of life. This ministry is not the individual Christian's ministry; it is the ministry of the body of Christ, because it is indeed Christ's ministry.

Anderson builds on this notion that we are joining Christ in his ministry and provides a unique way to look at the direction of our calling. Although we have been told to understand and discuss calling in terms of something earthward that we have been called to—pastoral ministry, motherhood, India, personal passions and desires, peacemaking, a job that satisfies one's soul, and so on—Anderson reverses the direction of our calling. He says,

> The on-going ministry of Jesus Christ gives both content and direction to the Church in its ministry. Jesus is the minister *par excellence*. He ministers to the Father for the sake of the world. . . . The church has no existence apart from being called into being through this ministry and equipped for it by the gift of the Holy Spirit. . . . The Holy Spirit unites the doing of ministry to the ministry which has already been accomplished in Christ. . . . As Christ's own ministry is unfolded and proclaimed, the Church discovers its own ministry, and its members their own particular ministry. Christ continually discloses his ministry in concrete situations. This disclosure is the source of all true innovation and creativity in ministry.[66]

Reversing how we envision the direction of our calling is critical for engaging in ministry, both inside and outside the local church, further reinforcing the reality that no ministry is truly one's own but is instead Christ's ministry. We are called to participate in Christ, specifically in the tangible expressions of his ministry in the world. To summarize, calling centers on the Christian's participation in Christ, a participation that is corporate in nature. This establishes the nature of calling: the church is in Christ, in and for the world.

66. Anderson, "Theology for Ministry," 8.

So, how does this look at the individual level? How do we understand the implications of our corporate calling to Christ, which is manifested in concrete situations in the whole of the Christian's life? To this we now turn our attention: the nature of Christian identity and personhood because of our corporate calling in Christ.

Calling and the Individual Believer

Since our calling is to Christ and to participate in his ongoing ministry in the world, how then should individual Christians understand their own identity as part of the called people of God? And how do Christians live faithfully in keeping with their calling in Christ? To start answering these questions, we return to Newbigin, who said that in Christ "we are a new creation, *a new humanity.*"[67] When a person is in Christ, they are still *physically* the same person, but *spiritually* and therefore theologically they are now able to live into the fullness of their humanity as one made in the image of God. Dorothy Sayers recognized that there was something unique about how God formed people to be creators, just as God is a creator. In her words, "Man is a maker, who makes things because he wants to, because he cannot fulfill his true nature if he is prevented from making things for the love of the job. He is made in the image of the Maker, and he must himself create or become something less than man."[68] Being human extends beyond the fact that one has a physical body. There is something quite human about working and putting our hands to some task through our work in every realm of life. This work extends far beyond the activities one does for gainful employment. Sayers observes, "We can measure the distance we have fallen from the idea that work is a vocation to which we are called, by the extent to which we have

---

67. Newbigin, *Household of God*, 36, emphasis added.
68. Sayers, "Vocation in Work," 406. Sayers here uses "man" generically to mean "human beings."

come to substitute the word 'employment' for 'work.'"[69] Sayers understood the relationship between being human and being a worker, but she also recognized the danger of conflating one's calling with one's work.

It is no coincidence that adult workers tend to find their identity in their work, and they often associate their calling with a particular kind of work. When calling and work are conflated, one's identity becomes entangled with their work. If we come to understand our work as our calling, we become what we do. But this should not be so for believers, for our *calling in Christ is our identity-forming reality*. The Christian's calling is rooted in one's participation in Christ. This participation is not simply about the individual Christian and Christ, but rather about the individual's incorporation into the church, which is the corporate Christ.

Considered through a christological and ecclesial lens, the Christian's identity is not primarily about one's individual agency in the world, contrary to so much current popular thinking.[70] Grant Macaskill argues that the Christian's agency in the world should focus not on performing moral acts or becoming a better version of oneself but on "becoming someone else," and that someone is Christ.[71] Macaskill points out that too much emphasis has been placed on Christians asking, "What would Jesus do?" As a result, believers have failed to recognize that the NT writers "represent Christian moral identity *principally* as inhabitation rather than imitation."[72] The Christian life and therefore the Christian's identity is not about making right choices, having a certain type of job, or finding one's passion; instead, it is about being "united to Christ, clothed

69. Sayers, "Vocation in Work," 409.
70. See Taylor, *Sources of the Self*.
71. Macaskill, *Living in Union with Christ*, 26.
72. Macaskill, *Living in Union with Christ*, 36. This does not mean that imitation is unimportant for the Christian. Paul does affirm the importance of imitation (1 Cor. 11:1), but imitation is a result of inhabitation by Christ.

with Christ, baptized into Christ, and [abiding] in Christ."[73] For Macaskill, being in Christ is "the most basic category of Christian identity."[74]

Our in-Christ-calling identity thus colors and shapes everything we put our hands to, regardless of whether there is monetary remuneration for the activity, whether there is a personal sense of passion for the activity, or even whether it is what one feels "wired" to do. Calling is so much larger than one's work or ministry or passion. There is certainly a relationship between calling and activity, but any activity must spring from our identity in Christ, not the other way around. Based on Paul's writings, Michael Gorman puts it this way: "Because Paul expects the church to embody the gospel, to become the gospel, its very identity is inherently missional."[75] So how does our identity influence the ways we engage God's mission in the world? Our calling to Christ helps us understand who we are, which then informs what, how, and why we do all things in life. Rather than emphasize *doing* something because we are supposedly called to it, we should emphasize *being* a certain sort of people who are in Christ and marked by holiness, peace, justice, love, and other Christlike characteristics. Instead of a "be-all-you-can-be" narrative, we have the opportunity to live a "be-all-that-Christ-is-in-the-world" narrative. Our identity as individuals is not tied to a particular job, task, subjective feeling, or role but is instead tethered to Christ. Gordon Smith observes, "Our vision for the Christian life is not merely that we would be formed into the image of Christ—that we would be like Christ Jesus. Rather, the extraordinary vision into which we are called is that we would be drawn into the very life of Christ and thereby into the life of God. Our vision and

---

73. Macaskill, *Living in Union with Christ*, 36. Making a connection between landmarks 1 and 2 later in this chapter, Macaskill locates this Christ-inhabitation within the community of believers: "'In Christ' is really just a way of saying 'in the church that imitates Christ.'"

74. Macaskill, *Living in Union with Christ*, 41.

75. Gorman, *Becoming the Gospel*, 18.

passion is union with Christ."[76] Smith's point brings us back to where we began this theological reflection on calling—union and participation with Christ.

Theological Landmarks for Calling

To summarize our klesiology by using the map metaphor we began with, we propose three theological landmarks that will serve to reorient us to a faithful use and application of calling terminology. These landmarks grow out of the preceding biblical and theological investigations. They also address the concerns that Volf raises regarding Luther's understanding of work as vocation, safeguarding us from getting too far off the road as we apply our understanding of calling in the real world.

Calling Is Participation in Christ

There is no primary versus secondary calling designation in the Bible. This landmark helps dispel the ambiguity regarding Luther's internal versus external calling designations critiqued by Volf (see above). Our calling to Christ is not our primary calling: it *is* our calling. To conflate our calling with anything other than who we are in Christ is to supplant the preeminence of our union with Christ with something that is far inferior. This landmark helps Christians navigate the complexity and challenge of having multiple jobs or no job at various points in their lives, the ever-shifting nature of today's workforce that often requires multiple changes in job or career, the fact that aging affects one's ability to engage in the same work performed in earlier years, and the reality that one may not have passions available to pursue. Even though these realities and many others occur, one's calling to participate in Christ does not change and indeed remains the same despite life's shifting circumstances.

76. G. Smith, *Called to Be Saints*, 41–42.

Calling Is Corporate before It Is Individual

Rather than start with *me*, we need to start with *we*. This does not minimize or eliminate the importance of the individual. Instead, it locates the individual within a corporate matrix rather than in isolation. Such a directional move will force individuals to see themselves as part of a web with others, which reinforces what Paul communicated to the churches. This landmark will also safeguard us from wrongly justifying unhealthy and oppressive work environments for those alienated in their work, as we saw above in Volf's critique of Luther (and in some of the downsides we observed in chap. 1). It also gives those working in unhealthy and oppressive work environments a faithful way forward (holiness in Christ), even when the work itself is not dignifying.

Calling Frames the Individual Christian's Identity in Terms of Who They Are rather than What They Do

Rather than building an identity around a job, task, or ministry, Christians see their identity through the lens of who they are in Christ. They seek to reflect Christ to the world through the way they live—with humility, love, kindness, and other Christlike characteristics. This landmark safeguards the Christian from wandering into the desert of work-as-idolatry, as we saw above in Volf's sixth critique of Luther. Work is important, but it is not the most valuable aspect of a person's identity. Some people do not have jobs or cannot work, but their identity in Christ continues. What gives identity and agency to Christians is first and foremost who they are in Christ, through whom they were created for good works that he has prepared for them (Eph. 2:10). Any job, task, or role that a Christian assumes should not be elevated above the rightful place that Christ holds as creator, sustainer, and identity-framer. Work is a context in the Christian's life where they can pursue good deeds and reflect Christ to the world, but this is an avenue for expressing their identity *in Christ* and not what forms their identity.

In some ways this third theological landmark on our calling map leads us back to the first. It creates an important theological loop that must undergird and inform our understanding of calling, thus providing the theological framework for God's people to experience freedom and unity together *in Christ*. This reframing of calling brings freedom because Christians are able to freely express who they are in Christ regardless of their circumstances, no matter how ideal or challenging their circumstances may be. This reframing of Christian calling brings unity because there is no difference between Christians. Regardless of gender, ethnicity, economic status, age, or geography, we are all one in Christ, all have the same calling, and all must see each other as such.

Conclusion: Theology for Identity and Mission

After a theological exploration of calling and proposing these three theological landmarks on our calling map, two conclusions follow. First, our collective calling in Christ informs and undergirds our very understanding of what it means to be God's people. We express our calling through our individual lives, but only as we live faithfully in community with Christ and one another. As a result, our calling and identity go hand in hand. I am who I am in Christ; you are who you are in Christ; we are who we are in Christ. Second, this identity informs our understanding of what it means to participate in God's mission in the world. Our involvement in the mission of God is far more about who we are than what we do. Even if life changes through the loss of a job, the loss of a loved one, moving across the country or across town, or adjustments due to aging, our calling does not change or go away. As life changes, we have the opportunity to discern and explore new expressions of our calling to Christ within our new contexts and circumstances.

The tourists at the beginning of this chapter stubbornly pressed forward even when it was apparent that they were off course; for far too long, Christians likewise have pressed forward with an unhealthy view of calling. It is time that we pay attention to the proper theological landmarks in front of us, listen to the wise guides who have charted the course before us, and reorient ourselves toward a proper understanding and expression of our calling. This biblically anchored and theologically guided view of calling necessitates specific applications within our real-world circumstances. To this task we now turn.

6

The Road Ahead

Embracing Our Calling

To avoid compromising or minimizing the important place that "calling" ought to have in the lives of Christians and the church, we must avoid using some popular but incorrect terminology. To remain faithful to the biblical understanding of "calling," how might we best use this word? Where do we go from here?

First, in chapters 1 and 2 we looked at common uses of the word "calling." Although we discovered a range of uses with varying nuances among them, essentially three meanings predominate.

1. A calling refers to one's *job, task, or ministry*, whether this is in the religious or secular spheres. We saw, for example, how Luther championed the view that all jobs are callings from God. Others repeatedly urge people to make their jobs their callings or find their calling (usually defined "spiritually") embedded in their jobs. This encourages people to feel that they have significance and meaning in their daily work. In the religious realm, it is common to require that pastors, missionaries, or other ministry professionals have a

call from God. To put it differently, religious professionals or laypersons engaging in ministry activities need to discern a "call" as an indispensable component of their placement in ministry. Some religious bodies—whether on the denominational or congregational level—require a process for vetting candidates to ensure that they possess a "call," presumably a call from God to a particular ministry. The assumption here is that God calls people to work in specific jobs or roles.

2. A calling is one's individual *vocation*—variously described as a talent, yearning, aptitude, or passion and as what one was designed, gifted, or wired to do—regardless of whether one expresses that "calling" in a job. We saw repeated examples of authors or speakers urging people to find that sweet spot in which, as Buechner opines, our deep gladness meets the world's need.[1] Likewise, Brooks urges readers to discover the calling in them that requires dedication and sacrifice.[2]

3. One's calling waits to be discovered. One must search for one's calling since it may not be obvious and may require effort to uncover. Trial and error are often required. One may not sense one's calling for many years until a search finally reveals it. Or one may not be ready to notice it until certain factors open up or come together. Often this point follows from the first two points; many insist that one must search diligently to find that job or vocation in which their calling resides.

Why Is Calling Language Misused?

Without a doubt, people find many of the popular meanings for the term and concept of "calling" very attractive. Indeed, we find them everywhere. But do prevalence and attractiveness give us warrant to ignore this misuse of a word and the unfortunate

1. Buechner. *Wishful Thinking*, 95.
2. Brooks, *Second Mountain*, 103.

consequences that can potentially ensue? We authors would be foolish simply to dismiss the widespread use of these popular understandings or imagine that our book will convince all readers. As we noted earlier, people may use words to mean whatever they wish, and these interpretations of "call"—popularized by Buechner, Guinness, and Brooks, to mention only a few of those we cataloged in chapter 1—seem to resonate with and energize many people (and sell books). But it is fair to ask, especially of Christians, Why are these meanings of "call" so attractive and dominant despite our findings that they are not the meanings presented in the Bible or by responsible biblical theology? Several answers come to the surface.

In today's Western world in particular, people find significance in what they do and the outcomes they pursue. In one writer's formulation, we find meaning and significance in the "effective self" rather than the "bestowed self."[3] Popular self-help gurus like Anthony Robbins[4] or Steven Covey[5] (going all the way back to Norman Vincent Peale[6] and more recently the "prosperity gospel" in the Christian world) preach that effectiveness is a person's highest goal and demonstrates their worth. No wonder pursuit of a calling in these terms proves so attractive. Who would not want to be effective? Who would not seek after success? But when a person's worth or success is measured in these terms, we end up valuing a certain type of human agency and success more than others. Instead of "doing" and "being" existing in a dynamic relationship where each grows out of the other, "doing" eclipses "being" in this way of measuring our worth.

In a properly reflective life, "doing" and "being" will each inform the other. As Christians who grow in who we are (as God's holy ones in Christ), we will be more apt to "do" our jobs, tasks,

3. See, e.g., Woodhead, "Theology and the Fragmentation of the Self."
4. Robbins, *Unlimited Power.*
5. Covey, *Seven Habits of Highly Effective People.*
6. Peale, *Power of Positive Thinking.*

and roles with godly passion and purpose. And as we engage our jobs, tasks, and roles with this godly vigor, we will grow in holiness because we submit ourselves to what is truly the "call" of Christ on our lives. Although we have no desire to minimize the *doing* requirement of the gospel in any way, we need to be aware of the danger of allowing the culture to define what successful "doing" entails or what "effectiveness" means. Jesus valued the Samaritan because he loved his neighbor, which we have argued is part of our calling (being) in Christ, and this love led him to "do" extraordinary acts of charity (Luke 10:30–37). The widow gave her two copper coins because she loved God, as we are called to do in Christ, and her gift was no less significant despite its meager monetary value (Luke 21:1–4).

In addition, the prevailing narratives of our contemporary Western world champion the twin themes of "Do what you love" and "Follow your passion."[7] Such narratives build on the pervasiveness of individualism as an essential Western cultural value.[8] These stories about effectiveness and following one's *own* passion dominate how most people in the West function and evaluate their personal worth. It's a cliché that every high school commencement address urges graduates to be true to themselves and assures them that they can become anything they set their hearts to. Frank Sinatra croons so winsomely, "I did it my way," and people readily embrace that mantra. These story lines are influential in our culture, and they dominate even how Christians have come to assess their lives as followers of Christ. The Christian life becomes transactional. People prefer to function in a living-*for*-God paradigm rather than a living-*with*-God

---

7. For a helpful critique of this "passion narrative," see Newport, *So Good They Can't Ignore You.* He contends that this message for young people is bogus; they need to get to work and build skills. On the other hand, as we say repeatedly, many people will not find jobs or roles that they love doing, but they can do their jobs in ways that show how they love God.

8. For a thorough analysis and defense of individualism, see the groundbreaking book by Bellah et al., *Habits of the Heart.*

paradigm.[9] Again, for them "doing" outperforms "being." When Christians seek to craft "their best life" on these production values, they are susceptible to writers and speakers who tell them that this kind of life is their calling and in this way put a spiritual spin on the message.

Authors portray the successful Christian "calling" by *spiritualizing* the culture's values of effectiveness, passion, individualism, and a do-what-you-love narrative. As a result, reframing a Christian's "calling" in these terms seems convincing and appeals to a wide audience. What's more, serious Christians long to have an authoritative, if not divine, confirmation that they are making the correct choices in life, that they are pursuing the very paths that God has designed for them. Of course, this is a laudable motivation, but it becomes problematic when that path (now termed a "calling") is defined by the culture's values rather than by a robust biblical understanding. As a result, the biblical meaning of "calling" gets nudged aside or, more likely, co-opted. "Take up your cross and follow me" falls on deaf ears because we become unwilling to take up jobs or roles that we perceive as "beneath us" or inconvenient, ones that don't attract us. While this is not the place for a cultural analysis or deconstruction, we believe this cultural lens is a very narrow and selfish way to portray our calling in Christ.

It is equally troubling that many if not most Christians in the world do not have the luxury of discovering this redefined view of calling. Many are left behind or alienated if calling only equals a job that one can choose, love, or feel passion about. If calling is limited to the values of passion, individualism, and "fun," many Christians simply lose out because not all jobs are like this. Some jobs are downright hard to get out of bed for every day. While these difficult jobs might serve the needs of the world and put food on our tables, to suggest that we feel "passion" for them might only

9. See Jethani, *With*.

breed discouragement. How tragic if all Christians have a calling in Christ, but most never learn what that means!

The Way Forward in "The Call"

In this book, we have argued that the church would be better served if we employed calling language in ways that conform to how the NT uses it. A Christian's calling is not concealed like a needle in a haystack. All believers possess a calling that the Scriptures clearly present and explain. Buttressed with a rich knowledge of their calling, believers can flourish in all aspects of their lives. If we limit calling to a job, passion, or other narrow dimension of one's life, we diminish the Bible's robust theology of calling. What "calling" do all believers possess?

The Biblical Meanings for "Calling"

We discovered several dimensions of the normative meaning of "calling" for Christians today. The NT affirms the following five points.

1. Believers are called to salvation in Christ. Their fundamental *individual* identity is a "Christ one," a Christian. A follower of Christ is a called one.
2. Believers are called members of the church, the *corporate* body of Christ. Thus, to be "in Christ" not only establishes an individual identity but also joins each believer to the community that has a calling. The calling of Christians resides in their identity as members of the church, the body of Christ. As such, they are holy ones, God's people, and those loved by God.
3. Believers find their calling in Jesus's commission to his followers to perform certain tasks; they have a calling to engage in mission in Jesus's name. "Being" leads to "doing," and "doing"

reflects what we are becoming in Christ. At the core, Jesus's Great Commission (Matt. 28:18–20) summarizes the missional nature of our calling, though the NT writers outline other elements of our participation with God's mission in the world.

4. Believers are called to godly virtues and behaviors, the *character* of those in Christ. Their calling stipulates how the members of the church relate to each other and to the world. Jesus's Great Commandment (Matt. 22:37–40; Luke 10:27), loving God and neighbor, epitomizes their calling, though the NT writers present many dimensions of the qualities believers are called to possess and express. The slogan "Become What You Are" captures the Christian's calling.[10]

5. On the other hand, while Jesus established various offices and the requisite giftings for the functioning and building up of the church, Jesus *does not call specific individuals* to fill those roles.[11]

Embracing Our Calling as Christians

This leads us to offer the following principles for followers of Christ who wish to take seriously their calling in Christ. Our assumption is that believers understand and are seeking to live in light of the NT description of their call that we have just outlined. That is, they know their calling in Christ; they do not need to discover it. Here are some ways in which the called ones implement their "calling."

Individuals

1. If someone is seeking a specific job, occupation, or ministry, an interviewer should not confuse the issue by asking whether the

---

10. On unpacking this theme in Jesus's teaching in the Sermon on the Mount, see W. Klein, *Become What You Are*.

11. Here we are excluding the apostles, whom Jesus did specifically appoint to their office in the foundation of the church.

applicant has a "call" to pursue it. When people have the freedom and resources to pursue where to invest their lives in some ministry, whether as a paid job or a volunteer role, the ability to identify a "call" to that specific task may be neither here nor there. A subjective sense of call does not determine whether one ought to pursue an opportunity or its significance, and searching for one may prove to be futile and, we believe, unnecessary. One's *call as a Christian* determines the value of any particular venture, since it is a call that applies to all of life for every believer. So, for example, a pastor's or missionary's position is no less important if they cannot identify a "call" to pursue it. All pastors have a call, but so do all laypeople! Their calling is in Christ.

Recommendation. We recommend that the criteria for entering a job, occupation, or ministry should focus on one's gifts, skills, desire, experience, aptitude, and temperament, not whether one can identify a "call" to that position. Employing these objective criteria will enable a candidate and prospective employers to make appropriate assessments about whether an applicant fits and is qualified for a specific position. Conversely, if the criterion is limited to one of the popular meanings of "a call" (e.g., hearing a word from God, identifying an inner passion, confirmation by some authority figure or discerning committee), the process becomes much more subjective and susceptible to misjudgment and even manipulation. Failing to receive one of these popular types of "callings" may cause a sincere believer to miss an opportunity for which they are well suited.

On the other hand, if all Christians have a "calling," as we discovered in our biblical and theological studies, then every believer can with confidence and hope decide how they will live in that calling in all dimensions of their lives. "All Christians" of course includes the unemployed, the underemployed, those not earning livable wages, blue-collar workers, gig-economy workers, the incarcerated, those experiencing homelessness, retirees, and the disabled. It includes single moms, widowers, choir directors, school administrators, high schoolers, and members of Congress. *All Christians* have God's call on their lives, even though many of them have no freedom to "do it my way" or "find their inner passion." Who they are in Christ defines their calling, not what they do, not any job or the lack of one, and not the presence or absence of passion for their work.

With a biblical perspective on calling, all Christians have the freedom and obligation to live faithfully in all aspects of their lives—not, as popular views of calling maintain, merely in their jobs, ministries, and passions. Everything they are and do grows out of their calling in Christ. Not limited to certain "spiritual" arenas or vocational passions, calling takes over all of life. All sectors of life are avenues to show how Christians are called ones and what they are called to be and do. Imagine how this could shape the way Christian parents teach their children and explain what it means to be a Christian in the world. The sacred/secular divide no longer exists, for whatever occupation or vocation a child chooses becomes an opportunity to live as a called person.

Qualification. Nevertheless, we realize that job seekers, vocation pursuers, and religious entities will persist in employing calling language to determine whether one has the requisite call, despite the confusion and subjectivity this involves. Church or parachurch bodies will seek to determine whether a candidate has a call. Those looking for assurance that taking up a ministry position rests on God's initiative rather than their own will find it difficult to stop relying on a "spiritual" sense of call as this has been popularly understood. Our book will not overturn centuries of tradition! We are not advocating that religious bodies or individuals cease vetting candidates. We merely wish that they would stop using a candidate's sense of "call" as one of the qualifications for ministry.

2. If one is looking for a cause in which to invest one's life, one need not use calling language to denote it as worthy or personally validating. Many needs exist in the world around us. Opportunities

abound. There is no shortage of worthy enterprises. The range of options for engaging one's skills or interests is virtually limitless. Mentors and confidants can be invaluable in helping a person find what they're good at, but discovering what to pursue does not require a "call."

Recommendation. One can use language such as passion, commitment, desire, gifting, and the like to pinpoint the motivations to pursue a worthy cause, but employing calling language opens the door to confusion, particularly in the religious sphere (e.g., "God has called me to work on the problem of homelessness"). We suggest speaking of discovering your passion or what seems to be your intense interest, gifting, or wiring or how you can invest your life to meet a great need. If you want to join Sinatra's "I did it my way," that's okay. We are free to discern and use the gifts and talents God has given us. Just don't use the word "calling" for that pursuit. Use the word "vocation" if you must, but this is not what the NT means by "calling."

Qualification. We face another tall task if we authors think we can excise this popular use of calling from Christian discourse. We much prefer that people employ the term "vocation" for this use, because this helps to keep the meaning distinct from what the NT means by "calling." When the term "vocation" is distinguished from "calling," it avoids obscuring and confusing the biblical meaning.

3. The "hiddenness" of calling as popularly understood should be jettisoned. God's calling of Christians is not hidden at all; it is as plain as day on the pages of the NT. Armed with a proper biblical understanding, one's calling is not hidden; it is in Christ, and the NT clearly delineates its features. What may be "hidden" and need to be discovered, discerned, or developed are one's gifts, skills, desires, aptitudes, and temperament. Again, mentors, pastors, or wise friends can provide immeasurable help here. God will use all these as believers seek to follow their divine calling. The "calling" in Christ is clear enough; how and

where to practice that calling may require careful discernment and investigation.

Recommendation. We urge all Christians, in Paul's language, "to live a life worthy of the calling you have received" (Eph. 4:1).

The Church

Thinking corporately, we contend that several issues are paramount. First, since we are members of one body, the church, which has a calling from God, *unity* becomes an essential value and objective. For example, we saw that Paul characterizes the Corinthian church as the "called" or "called ones."[12] First Corinthians 1–3 especially stresses the importance of unity. In fact, division is inimical to the body of Christ, for Christ is not divided (1 Cor. 1:13; 10:17). Unity in the body of Christ is a pervasive and *central* theme in Paul's discussion of the church. His words ring out in clarion terms:

> As a prisoner for the Lord, then, I urge you to live a life worthy of the calling you have received. Be completely humble and gentle; be patient, bearing with one another in love. Make every effort to keep the unity of the Spirit through the bond of peace. There is one body and one Spirit, just as you were called to one hope when you were called; one Lord, one faith, one baptism; one God and Father of all, who is over all and through all and in all. (Eph. 4:1–6)

Inherent in the church's calling is the requirement for its unity.

At a time in our world when polarization into sparring factions seems prevalent in virtually every arena of life (think politics, Facebook, classes, races, etc.), members of Christ's church ought to demonstrate unity. Sadly, too often the church is not an exception to this polarization. Strife and divisions impugn the very essence of the church's calling to embody Christ in the world. People outside the church see as much divisiveness among Christians as

12. See 1 Cor. 1:2, 24, 26; cf. 7:15, 17–18, 20–22, 24.

they find anywhere else, if not more. If you wish to know what God is calling your church to become, the answer is not hidden. God calls his people to promote and work for unity within its own ranks and in the wider Christian world. Unity ought to prevail in two arenas: within each local church and among the wider body of Christians. Jesus prays to his Father that his people might be one (John 17:20–23). As believers called to unity, we can oppose hating and polarizing. We can honor our unique differences and admit our areas of disagreement while at the same time seeking unity in Christ.

Second, beyond individual churches, there may be an important implication here for larger Christian groupings such as denominations. We have two suggestions. One is to repeat the call to unity. See that unity prevails among the sister churches that have bound themselves together. But also pursue unity with other Christian bodies to demonstrate how our commitment to Christ and his call on our lives transcends the parties into which we have divided ourselves over the course of church history. What a testimony it would be if Christian bodies found ways to work together to pursue the virtues that constitute our calling.[13]

Another suggestion concerns how denominations vet candidates for ordained ministries, as we mentioned above. Nothing we said about misuses of the terminology "call to ministry" should be taken to mean that would-be candidates for various ministry positions should not be rigorously scrutinized for their fitness. Assessing a person's qualification for ministry is essential, and there are various tests and instruments for doing that. Our only recommendation is this: beyond those qualifications, do not require a statement of a divine "call" *to that specific ministry* as one of the essential criteria. Requiring such a "call" might put a candidate in an awkward position, for our study has shown that the NT

---

13. There is also a role for the church to pursue its calling in the larger world outside the church. We think of Jesus's call for his people to be peacemakers (Matt. 5:9) and to love their enemies (Matt. 5:43–47).

knows no such qualification. If you insist on using that terminology, give careful thought to how you measure it. Its absence might be irrelevant when the person possesses all the qualifications for a position as well as the traits the NT cites as part of God's call on all believers. If you have taken all necessary steps to vet candidates and you deem them worthy, then place them or hire them regardless of whether they can point to evidence of a divine call.

How We Understand and Speak about Ministry

In view of this, we would do well not to speak of ministry as a "calling." Calling, as we have seen, resides within each believer, no matter what their occupation, job, or "vocation"—whether secular or religious—and even if they are not employed. But when we misconstrue what "calling" means, we unnecessarily and indefensibly create a division that elevates some occupations as more worthy or spiritual than others. Laypeople feel inferior when they have not been "called" to be a missionary. How does one know if they have this call? Such use of calling language intensifies the sacred/secular or clergy/laity divide in ways that diminish the true calling that God gives to all believers. Certainly some roles within a church are more prominent than others.[14] We are not arguing against the place and function of vocational or paid Christian workers. In fact, a proper use of calling creates a greater obligation to see that mature and faithful Christians hold such offices. Although a pastor's role may involve more overtly in-church tasks than, say, an actuary's, as Christians they have the same "calling" in Christ. What is more, according to Paul all Christians are ministers (Eph. 4:12; cf. Rev. 2:19).

How Pastors View Their Work

Embracing this view of "call" in no way diminishes the crucial role of church staff workers—whether paid or unpaid, ordained or

---

14. Paul makes that point in discussing spiritual gifts (1 Cor. 12:15–31).

not—and those in other religious vocations, such as parachurch organizations. Our credentials for serving Christ reside not in an individual "call" but in the spiritual gifts, skills, experience, and other qualifications needed to perform a specific ministry. Removing specific "call to ministry" terminology in no way lessens a person's standing or credibility in their service for Christ. The potential gain is an increase in "recruits" who sincerely wish to serve Christ in one of these vocations but who cannot identify that elusive sense of call that they hear others speak about so confidently.

For those in formal pastoral and ministerial roles, the view of calling presented in this book will also help in two additional ways. First, it gives shape to how we equip those in the congregation for the work of ministry (Eph. 4:11–12). Since calling is about who we are in Christ rather than about a particular ministry task or role, all Christians should be affirmed by and within this calling. Being in Christ extends to the whole of life. Rather than use calling language to describe one's own position as a pastor or to compel volunteers to participate in specific ministry endeavors (such as short-term missions), pastors can and should affirm their congregants' calling in Christ and the varied implications of that calling in the whole of their lives. This includes their gainful employment; their pursuit of work if they are unemployed; their homes, neighborhoods, and cities; and the checkout line at their local grocery store. Emphasizing the Christian's calling in this way will inevitably increase the influence of the church in the world as each local church equips and sends people out to serve Christ in every avenue of their lives.

Second, drawing from Ray Anderson's thoughts regarding the direction of our calling (discussed in chap. 5 above), pastors ought to view their calling in terms of who they are in Christ rather than in terms of their position or job. They will then understand their pastoral ministry as an outgrowth of their identity rather than the totality of their identity. This adjusted perspective has significant implications. First, church ministry is a *part* of a pastor's faithful expression of their gifting, opportunities, and desires to serve Christ; it is not the *whole* of this expression. For many pastors, their church-related obligations functionally supersede other responsibilities. Instead, they should consider family, community, and other dimensions of their lives through the same calling lens as their pastoral obligations. The members of the local church, we hasten to add, also need to recognize this as the nature of their pastor's calling.

Second, no ministry is ever *the pastor's* ministry: it is *Christ's* ministry. We live in a time when many pastors see publishing and selling books, speaking at conferences, increasing their social media presence, and expanding their influence as indicators of success. At the same time, other pastors, perhaps serving in small churches or rural communities, feel they are inferior when they cannot use any of these metrics to demonstrate their success. A theology of calling changes the means used to measure success. When ministry is truly Christ's ministry, the pastor's ego, notoriety, and reputation are far less consequential (or should be). We can then evaluate the "success" of a pastor's ministry in terms of their faithfulness in Christlikeness (their true calling) rather than by the size of their following or reputation.

Third, change and flux are the norms more than ever before. Whether this happens as the active choice of the pastor or as a change imposed by people or circumstances outside the pastor's control (i.e., pastor loses a job, the church closes due to financial instability, or another occupational opportunity arises), when such significant change occurs, the pastor's calling remains the same: to Christ and a life of holiness. It can seem curious, if not pernicious, when a pastor suddenly announces to their current congregation a "call" to serve in another church. For when the language of "calling" is employed, the issue is settled and cannot be questioned. The bereft congregation can only lament and may actually resent God for calling a beloved pastor to serve elsewhere.

For this reason, we think it is better not to use call language to explain a pastoral move.

Seminaries and Christian Educational Institutions

That last point also has important implications for training institutions. Seminaries or religious colleges need not require or expect that students seeking to enter ministerial training programs possess a "call to ministry." This also holds true for denominational schools that may have strict requirements for ordination. There are many other qualifications to help discern a person's fitness for some college or seminary course of study without also requiring the elusive "call" to ministry. Students can be recruited as "volunteers for Jesus" even though they cannot articulate any clear occupational (i.e., religious vocational) direction. Theological training should enhance graduates' ability to follow God's "call" on their lives in the senses we have uncovered in our study here. Schools can "market" their programs as enabling students to fulfill the calling all believers have—to be and to become Christ's salt and light in the world.

As a result, the view of calling presented in this book necessitates that seminaries and religious colleges specifically and intentionally educate and equip Christian leaders to live lives of holiness, justice, peace, generosity, humility, kindness, and love. This does not mean that institutions of theological education should stop equipping students in other important subjects such as biblical and theological studies, leadership, liturgy, and ethics. However, formation in Christlikeness must be foundational and integrative rather than supplemental within the overall curriculum.

If Not a Call, Then What?

What is the appropriate language to use if we limit "calling" to its biblical senses? Though calling language is used in a slippery way for all kinds of actions, we think there are more suitable and appropriate ways to express these ideas. The following are examples of better verbiage along with some biblical examples that illustrate their uses. Rather than feeling obligated to say, "I am called," it is better to say one of the following phrases.

> *"I desire to pursue . . ."* In other words, what I want to engage in is a good thing, or fun, or useful, and I sincerely want to do it. For example, Paul affirms that *aspiring* to become an overseer in a church is a good thing (1 Tim. 3:1). He follows up that statement with qualifications that should be considered in vetting such an aspirant. Paul does not mention that the overseer must have a "call" from God to pursue that office.

> *"I feel compelled to . . ."* In other words, my commitment to Christ prods me to serve him in this way. For example, Paul affirmed, "I am compelled to preach" (1 Cor. 9:16). He felt an inner coercion to proclaim the gospel. He did not use calling language for this function of his ministry. People may well sense a strong inner urge to take on a task, and this is a worthy motivation. It parallels the language people use to describe finding what they are "wired" to do. Better to say, "I'm wired to do this," than to say, "I've found my calling."

> *"I want to . . ."* In other words, "I see this need that I am equipped to meet, and I have the time, resources, and inclination to do it." For example, some might use this wording when deciding to work with Habitat for Humanity to build houses for the needy. By the way, this grows out of their "calling" to love their neighbor. Their "calling" opens possibilities for service, but working for Habitat is not the calling. Equally a person might say, "I sense an obligation to give money to Food Bank of the Rockies to meet a need" (again, because of their "calling" to love their neighbors). A

Christian is called to love; giving money to meet a need is not a calling. Because Christians are called in Christ, they should ponder over how to be good stewards of their resources, not wait for a "calling" to give to some appeal.[15]

"*I have to do . . .*" For some people, whether they want to engage in a particular task or not, they simply must do it. To do it is not a calling; it is a necessity. For example, people need to work at all kinds of jobs to feed their families, regardless of whether that job is fulfilling to them or meets some laudable goal; in fact, the job may be distasteful, tedious, or otherwise unwelcome. For a believer, the *quality* of their work reflects their character (which grows out of their calling), but the job itself is not a calling.[16] For this reason, washing windows (or substitute many other occupations here) is a job; it is not a calling. To stay with this example, why wash windows? A believer's calling is to love our neighbor as ourselves, and this requires finding ways to feed the kids!

"*I must obey . . .*" This phrasing fits closely with the prior statement. For example, because of their position in Christ, the "called" must obey a *valid* requirement of a government or employer (emphasis on the word *valid*). Paul tells the Roman believers to "submit to the authorities" and pay taxes (Rom. 13:5–6). For Paul, such submission is a matter of conscience, expressing who we are in Christ. Submission is not a calling; it is what called people do out of reverence for Christ (Eph. 5:21; cf. 1 Pet. 2:13, 18). *Properly understood* submission is inherent in their calling.

---

15. Paul outlines some of these principles for giving in 2 Cor. 8–9. For a thorough appraisal of biblical teaching on stewardship, see Blomberg, *Christians in an Age of Wealth*.

16. Paul instructs slaves to do their labor sincerely and with integrity (see Eph. 6:5–8). Sincere labor with integrity is what slaves are "called" to because they are in Christ. Their "job" as a slave is not their calling.

"Downsides" No More

In chapter 1 we presented some downsides to the popular uses of calling language in the Christian culture. In conclusion, let us return to those case studies to see what improvements have been made.

1. Calling is to a job or role. Sarah Sanders claimed that God called Donald Trump to become president, and that is why he was elected. On the religious side, many claim that God calls pastors or other religious professionals to serve in their roles. Thus whoever can convince a congregation (or calling committee) of that call can be inducted into the position. In other words, God calls people to work in specific jobs or roles.

With a proper grasp of the calling that all Christians have as individuals and as members of the called body (the church), jobs are not callings—whether secular or religious. Calling resides in who we are as followers of Christ. All Jesus's followers without exception have the same calling. For all of us, the question becomes: How can I embrace my calling in every dimension of my life?

2. A sense of calling is subjective. How does one know when it is present, especially when it is a requirement for some ministry positions? In fact, it can be imagined, conjured up, misrepresented, or misconstrued. What happens to that sense of calling when the ministry to which one was "called" falls flat, or one fails in performing that job, or one is unfairly fired from a role? What happened to the call? Was there really no call to begin with, or can the call be rescinded or shelved for a time? If one can articulate this call (in whatever way), shouldn't that guarantee a job? One would think so if the call originated from God.

A Christian's calling is not subjective after all. It is not hidden and needing to be meticulously or prayerfully discerned. Every believer's calling is clearly portrayed in the NT; we don't need to "discover" it. Each Christian simply needs to embrace it and live it faithfully in all areas of life.

3. Those who can identify a call can enter occupations that are explicitly in the ministry category, such as pastors, missionaries, Christian educators, monks, and other Christian workers. The ministries of all other Christians are inherently inferior (though no one would dare to say this) because they lack a call from God.

Such a dichotomy based on calling language is found nowhere in the NT. There are different offices in the church, just as there are differing gifts of the Spirit to the members of Christ's body. All members of Christ's body have equal worth based on their common call to and in Christ. No call sets some believers over or apart from other ones. On the basis of misunderstanding the concept of "call," someone in the church may say "I am an eye, and I have no need of you, since you're only a hand" and diminish the significance of another.[17] But Paul repudiates such an appraisal, which denies how the NT understands the call that all believers share in common.

4. Everyone's work is a vocation or calling from God. To counter the dichotomous thinking and insistence on ministry hierarchy described in point 3, Christians are encouraged to find significance and meaning in their daily work. This seems laudable, but it is hard to put this positive spin on many mundane occupations. What about the homeless, unemployed, underemployed, those in unhealthy work environments, meat packers, or gig-economy workers? Despite how they try, many Christians simply cannot perceive any calling in what they do.

They are correct. Calling is not found in one's job or other life circumstances. Finding worth and significance is crucial, and it is to be found in how the NT defines calling, not in a job or task. Christians find fulfillment and significance in their *being* in Christ and in how understanding who they are shapes how they live.

5. There are inherent ambiguities in some uses of the term "calling" that can lead to abuses, intentional or not. People are

17. Paraphrasing Paul's point in 1 Cor. 12:21.

recruited to ministries based on false claims such as "If you don't have a calling to stay in the US, God is calling you to foreign missions."[18] A "call" to missions is glamorized as God's best for our lives. Such guilt trips may coerce sincere Christians into taking positions they are not qualified for. When people cannot get along with their coworkers in some ministry, or church attendance is declining, or an offer comes from a larger church, God conveniently "calls" them to serve elsewhere! For example, why is it typically the pastor who informs a congregation of a "call" to leave, yet the congregation has no opportunity to confirm that they have heard this same call for a change in pastoral leadership? The local congregation is often left in the lurch. The problem lies in this misappropriation of the term "call" and its perceived unassailability. After all, who can question God's call? While we may fault those who manipulate and misuse the term, the popular and ambiguous sense of calling lends itself to such abuses.

Why not trash all this ambiguous and misleading language? To take a robust understanding of call and use the word in ways that serve questionable interests is unforgiveable. There are valid ways to impart to sincere Christians an understanding of God's mission in the world and encourage them to see whether they fit the criteria for a particular position without loading the conversation with the pious-sounding or guilt-inducing language of "call." A pastor can find honest and transparent ways to explain a move without resorting to the unassailable trump card of "God's call."

Parting Shot

Have you ever noticed that when you buy a particular item— perhaps a specific type of camera or model of automobile— suddenly you see them everywhere? For example, you never noticed how many Nissan Rogues are out there on the road until you or

---

18. What a lie, or at best a distortion of anything in the Bible!

someone you know gets one. Now that you are sensitized to it, stop and listen to how often people use calling language in church or religious circles as well as in the surrounding culture. To use a fancy word, it is ubiquitous; everyone talks about "calling." And let's face it, people use "call" and calling language in any way they please, as chapter 1 demonstrated. Our fond hope is that because of reading this book, *you* will begin to use it correctly. Is that an audacious goal? Perhaps, but we believe that the church has much to gain if every Christian understands and eagerly pursues their calling in Christ as the NT defines it and is freed from fretting because they don't seem to have a "calling" as others use the word. We end with what we hope are some words of wisdom.

A conversation about the nature of calling should remind us that we must allow the message of Scripture to speak into and challenge culture. Although we cannot escape our own context and the varied ways in which our culture influences us, our discussion of calling in this book reveals that we are sometimes (maybe often) far too easily influenced by the evolving trends around us. Nevertheless, the Bible is our compass, directing us back on course as it indicates true north. Let's use calling language the way Scripture uses it, which will spare us and others the downsides from false uses.

At a time when divisions run rampant within our broader culture and even within and among various churches, anchoring our common calling in Christ is a crucial step toward unity. As Christians, we profess to be part of the same body, but functionally we are deeply divided in many aspects of life (i.e., politics, race, economic status, theological positions, etc.). Getting *calling* right will not bridge every divide, but it will give us common ground to stand on as we strive to address our differences. After all, we are all pursuing the same calling. In 1 Corinthians Paul stressed this unifying call to that divided congregation, so what do we have to lose?

Seeing our calling as centered in Christ rather than a personalized job, task, role, or passion helps remove ego from the equation.

Christ sets the terms for how we are to live our lives. The Sermon on the Mount (Matt. 5–7) and other Scripture passages remind us of how Jesus wants his followers to live. At his departure, Jesus exhorted his followers to disciple the nations, which involves "teaching them to obey everything I have commanded you" (Matt. 28:20). To live this way is our calling; it is what Christ calls all believers to embrace. It is not hidden or difficult to discern, but the called life requires obedience and humility to affirm and live out.

We let the apostle Peter have the final word: "His divine power has given us everything we need for a godly life through our knowledge of him who *called* us by his own glory and goodness. . . . Therefore, my brothers and sisters, make every effort to confirm *your calling* and election. For if you do these things, you will never stumble, and you will receive a rich welcome into the eternal kingdom of our Lord and Savior Jesus Christ" (2 Pet. 1:3, 10–11, emphasis added).

Bibliography

Allen, Jason K. *Discerning Your Call to Ministry: How to Know and What to Do about It.* Chicago: Moody, 2016.

Anderson, Ray S. *On Being Human: Essays in Theological Anthropology.* Eugene, OR: Wipf & Stock, 2010.

———. *The Soul of Ministry: Forming Leaders for God's People.* Louisville: Westminster John Knox, 1997.

———. "A Theology for Ministry." In *Theological Foundations for Ministry: Selected Readings for a Theology of the Church in Ministry*, edited by Ray S. Anderson, 6–21. Edinburgh: T&T Clark, 1979.

Anselm. *Anselm of Canterbury: The Major Works.* Edited by Brian Davies and G. R. Evans. New York: Oxford University Press, 1998.

Augustine [of Hippo]. *Confessions and Enchiridion.* Edited by Albert C. Outler. Philadelphia: Westminster, 1955.

Barnes, Kenneth J. *Redeeming Capitalism.* Grand Rapids: Eerdmans, 2018.

Barth, Karl. *The Doctrine of Creation.* Vol. III/4 of *Church Dogmatics.* Edited by G. W. Bromiley and T. F. Torrance. New York: T&T Clark, 2009.

———. *The Doctrine of Reconciliation.* Vol. IV/3.2 of *Church Dogmatics.* Edited by G. W. Bromiley and T. F. Torrance. New York: T&T Clark, 2010.

Baxter, Richard. "Directions about Our Labor and Callings." In Placher, *Callings*, 278–85.

BBC News. "Selfie Deaths: 259 People Reported Dead Seeking the Perfect Picture." October 4, 2018. https://www.bbc.com/news/newsbeat-45745982.

Beale, G. K. *The Temple and the Church's Mission: A Biblical Theology of the Dwelling Place of God*. Downers Grove, IL: InterVarsity, 2004.

Bellah, Robert, et al. *Habits of the Heart*. New York: HarperCollins, 1985.

Blomberg, Craig L. *Christians in an Age of Wealth: A Biblical Theology of Stewardship*. Grand Rapids: Zondervan, 2013.

Bock, Darrell L. *Acts*. Baker Exegetical Commentary on the New Testament. Grand Rapids: Baker Academic, 2007.

Bonhoeffer, Dietrich. *Ethics*. Vol. 6 of Dietrich Bonhoeffer Works. Edited by Clifford J. Green. Translated by Reinhard Krauss, Charles C. West, and Douglas W. Stott. Minneapolis: Fortress, 2009.

Bourke, Dale Hanson. *Embracing Your Second Calling: Find Passion and Purpose for the Rest of Your Life*. Nashville: Thomas Nelson, 2009.

Brooks, David. *The Second Mountain. The Quest for a Moral Life*. New York: Random House, 2019.

Buechner, Frederick. *Wishful Thinking: A Theological ABC*. New York: Harper & Row, 1973.

Calvin, John. *Calvin's Institutes*. Abridged ed. Edited by Donald K. McKim. Louisville: Westminster John Knox, 2001.

———. *Institutes of the Christian Religion*. Translated by Robert White. Carlisle, PA: Banner of Truth Trust, 2017.

Campbell, Constantine R. *Paul and Union with Christ: An Exegetical and Theological Study*. Grand Rapids: Zondervan Academic, 2012.

Ciampa, Roy E., and Brian S. Rosner. *The First Letter to the Corinthians*. Pillar New Testament Commentaries. Grand Rapids: Eerdmans, 2010.

Covey, Steven R. *Seven Habits of Highly Effective People*. London: Simon & Schuster, 1989.

Downen, Robert, Lise Olsen, and John Tedesco. "Abuse of Faith: 20 Years, 700 Victims: Southern Baptist Sexual Abuse Spreads as Leaders Resist Reforms." *Houston Chronicle*, February 10, 2019. https://www.houston chronicle.com/news/investigations/article/Southern-Baptist-sexual-abuse -spreads-as-leaders-13588038.php.

Evans, G. R., ed. *The Medieval Theologians: An Introduction to Theology in the Medieval Period*. Malden, MA: Blackwell, 2001.

Fee, Gordon D. *The First Epistle to the Corinthians*. Rev. ed. New International Commentary on the New Testament. Grand Rapids: Eerdmans, 2014.

Feintzeig, Rachel. "Do You Dare Switch Jobs in the Coronavirus Economy?" *Wall Street Journal*, July 12, 2020. https://www.wsj.com/articles/do-you -dare-switch-jobs-in-the-coronavirus-economy-11594546200.

Friesen, Garry. *Decision Making and the Will of God*. Rev. and updated ed. Colorado Springs, CO: Multnomah, 2004.

Goins, Jeff. "How to Find Your Calling (and Why Most People Get This Wrong)." *Relevant Magazine*, August 27, 2013. https://relevantmagazine .com/life5/how-find-your-calling-and-why-most-people-get-wrong/.

Gorman, Michael. *Becoming the Gospel: Paul, Participation, and Mission*. Grand Rapids: Eerdmans, 2015.

———. *Participating in Christ: Explorations in Paul's Theology and Spirituality*. Grand Rapids: Baker Academic, 2019.

Gregory the Great. *The Book of Pastoral Rule*. Translated and introduced by George E. Demacopoulos. New York: St Vladimir's Seminary Press, 2007.

Guinness, Os. *The Call: Finding and Fulfilling the Central Purpose of Your Life*. Nashville: Thomas Nelson, 2003.

Haanen, Jeff. "God of the Second Shift: The Theology of Work Conversation Is Thriving; Why Are Most Workers Missing from It?" *Christianity Today* 62 (2018): 34–41.

Hagy, Jessica. "20 Ways to Find Your Calling." *Forbes*, June 26, 2012. https:// www.forbes.com/sites/jessicahagy/2012/06/26/20-ways-to-find-your -calling/#6499c4785b7d.

Hale, Lori Brandt. "Bonhoeffer's Christological Take on Vocation." In *Bonhoeffer, Christ and Culture*, edited by Keith L. Johnson and Timothy Larson, 175–90. Downers Grove, IL: IVP Academic, 2013.

Hamilton, Isobel Asher, and Aine Cain. "Amazon Warehouse Employees Speak Out about the 'Brutal' Reality of Working during the Holidays, When 60-Hour Weeks Are Mandatory and Ambulance Calls Are Common." *Business Insider*, February 19, 2019. https://www.businessinsider .com/amazon-employees-describe-peak-2019-2.

Harper, Brad, and Paul Louis Metzger. *Exploring Ecclesiology: An Evangelical and Ecumenical Introduction*. Grand Rapids: Brazos, 2009.

Harvey, Dave. *Am I Called? The Summons to Pastoral Ministry*. Wheaton: Crossway, 2012.

Heinecken, Martin J. "Luther and the 'Orders of Creation' in Relation to a Doctrine of Work and Vocation." *Lutheran Quarterly* 4 (1952): 393–414.

Hillman, James. *The Soul's Code: In Search of Character and Calling*. New York: Random House, 1996.

Holmes, Michael W., ed. and trans. *The Apostolic Fathers: Greek Texts and English Translations*. 3rd ed. Grand Rapids: Baker Academic, 2007.

Houston Chronicle. "A Chronicle Investigation: Abuse of Faith." June 2019. https://www.houstonchronicle.com/local/investigations/abuse -of-faith/.

Huie, Jessica. *Purpose: Find Your Truth and Embrace Your Calling*. New York: Hay House, 2018.

Isay, Dave. *Callings: The Purpose and Passion of Work*. New York: Penguin Books, 2016.

Jethani, Skye. *With: Reimagining the Way You Relate to God*. Nashville: Nelson, 2011.

Jones, Beth Felker. *Practicing Christian Doctrine: An Introduction to Thinking and Living Theologically*. Grand Rapids: Baker Academic, 2014.

Keller, Timothy, and Katherine Leary Alsdorf. *Every Good Endeavor: Connecting Your Work to God's Work*. New York: Riverhead Books, 2012.

Kittelson, James M., and Hans H. Wiersma. *Luther the Reformer: The Story of the Man and His Career*. Minneapolis: Fortress, 2016.

Klein, Matthew C. "The Coronavirus Hasn't Spared White Collar Jobs." *Barron's*, May 17, 2020. https://www.barrons.com/articles/software-engineers -consultants-dentists-the-coronavirus-hasnt-spared-white-collar-workers -51589367604.

Klein, William W. *Become What You Are: Spiritual Formation according to the Sermon on the Mount*. Downers Grove, IL: InterVarsity, 2006.

———. "Can You Worship Anyplace? Reflections on How the New Testament Answers the Question." *Midwestern Journal of Theology* 9 (2010): 96–121.

———. *The New Chosen People: A Corporate View of Election*. Rev. and exp. ed. Eugene, OR: Wipf & Stock, 2015.

———. "Paul's Use of *kalein*: A Proposal." *Journal of the Evangelical Theological Society* 27 (1984): 53–64.

Klein, William W., Craig L. Blomberg, and Robert L. Hubbard Jr. *Introduction to Biblical Interpretation*. 3rd ed. Grand Rapids: Zondervan, 2017.

Kolb, Robert. "Called to Milk Cows and Govern Kingdoms: Martin Luther's Teaching on the Christian's Vocations." *Concordia Journal* 39 (2013): 133–41.

———. "God Calling, 'Take Care of My People': Luther's Concept of Vocation in the Augsburg Confession and Its Apology." *Concordia Journal* 8 (1982): 4–11.

Kreider, Alan. *The Patient Ferment of the Early Church: The Improbable Rise of Christianity in the Roman Empire.* Grand Rapids: Baker Academic, 2016.

Kuzmič, Rhys. "*Beruf* and *Berufung* in Karl Barth's *Church Dogmatics*: Toward a Subversive Klesiology." *International Journal of Systematic Theology* 7 (2005): 262–78.

Labberton, Mark. *Called: The Crisis and Promise of Following Jesus Today.* Downers Grove, IL: InterVarsity, 2014.

Law, William. "A Serious Call to a Devout and Holy Life." In Placher, *Callings*, 303–10.

Lee, Daniel D. "Reading Scripture in Our Context: Double Particularity in Karl Barth's Actualistic View of Scripture." In *The Voice of God in the Text of Scripture*, edited by Oliver D. Crisp and Fred Sanders, 164–80. Grand Rapids: Zondervan, 2016.

Levoy, Gregg Michael. *Callings: Finding and Following an Authentic Life.* New York: Harmony, 1998.

Luther, Martin. *Commentaries on 1 Corinthians 7, 1 Corinthians 15, Lectures on 1 Timothy.* Edited by Hilton C. Oswald. Vol. 28 of *Luther's Works*. Saint Louis: Concordia, 1973.

———. *Lectures on Galatians (1535): Chapters 5–6.* Translated and edited by Jaroslav Pelikan. Vol. 27 of *Luther's Works*. St. Louis: Concordia, 1964.

Lynch, Joseph H., and Philip C. Adamo. *The Medieval Church: A Brief History.* 2nd ed. New York: Routledge, 2014.

Macaskill, Grant. *Living in Union with Christ: Paul's Gospel and Christian Moral Identity.* Grand Rapids: Baker Academic, 2019.

MacCulloch, Diarmaid. *Christianity: The First Three Thousand Years.* New York: Viking, 2010.

Marty, Martin. *Martin Luther.* New York: Viking, 2004.

"Martyrdom of Perpetua and Felicity, The." In *The Acts of the Christian Martyrs*, translated by Herbert Musurillo, 106–31. Acts of the Pagan and Christian Martyrs 2. Oxford: Clarendon, 1972.

McGrath, Alister E. *A Life of John Calvin: A Study in the Shaping of Western Culture.* Cambridge: Blackwell, 1990.

Miccoli, Giovanni. "Monks." In *Medieval Callings*, edited by Jacques Le Goff and translated by Lydia G. Cochrane, 37–73. Chicago: University of Chicago Press, 1996.

Migliore, Daniel L. *Faith Seeking Understanding: An Introduction to Christian Theology*. 3rd ed. Grand Rapids: Eerdmans, 2014.

Milton, Michael A. *Called? Pastoral Guidance for the Divine Call to Gospel Ministry*. Ross-Shire, Scotland: Christian Focus, 2018.

Nelson, Tom. *Work Matters: Connecting Sunday Worship to Monday Work*. Wheaton: Crossway, 2011.

Newbigin, Lesslie. *The Household of God: Lectures on the Nature of the Church*. Eugene, OR: Wipf & Stock, 2008.

———. *Truth to Tell: The Gospel as Public Truth*. Grand Rapids: Eerdmans, 1991.

Newport, Cal. *So Good They Can't Ignore You: Why Skills Trump Passion in the Quest for Work You Love*. New York: Grand Central Publishing, 2012.

Ocejo, Richard E. *Masters of Craft: Old Jobs in the New Urban Economy*. Princeton: Princeton University Press, 2017.

Ottaway, Alison. "10 Strategies for Gradually Figuring Out Your 'Life's Calling.'" *Mind Body Green*, June 29, 2020. https://www.mindbodygreen .com/0-7474/10-ways-to-uncover-your-true-calling.html.

Padilla, Kristen. *Now That I'm Called: A Guide for Women Discerning a Call to Ministry*. Grand Rapids: Zondervan, 2018.

Peale, Norman Vincent. *The Power of Positive Thinking*. New York: Prentice-Hall, 1952.

Perkins, William. "A Treatise of the Vocations." In Placher, *Callings*, 262–73.

Pew Research Center. "The State of American Jobs: How the Shifting Economic Landscape Is Reshaping Work and Society and Affecting the Way People Think about the Skills and Training They Need to Get Ahead." October 6, 2016. https://www.pewsocialtrends.org/2016/10/06/the-state -of-american-jobs/.

Placher, William, ed. *Callings: Twenty Centuries of Christian Wisdom on Vocation*. Grand Rapids: Eerdmans, 2005.

Raynor, Jordan. *Called to Create: A Biblical Invitation to Create, Innovate, and Risk*. Grand Rapids: Baker Books, 2017.

Riffkin, Rebecca. "In U.S., 55% of Workers Get Sense of Identity from Their Job." Gallup: Politics, August 22, 2014. https://news.gallup.com /poll/175400/workers-sense-identity-job.aspx.

Robbins, Anthony. *Unlimited Power: The New Science of Personal Achievement*. New York: Simon & Schuster, 1988.

Roper, Lyndal. *Martin Luther: Renegade and Prophet*. New York: Random House, 2017.

Sayers, Dorothy. *Letters to a Diminished Church: Passionate Arguments for the Relevance of Christian Doctrine*. Nashville: Nelson, 2004.

———. "Vocation in Work." In Placher, *Callings*, 405–12. Earlier published in *A Christian Basis for the Post-War World*, edited by A. E. Baker, 89–105. New York: Morehouse-Gorham, 1942.

Schuurman, Douglas J. *Vocation: Discerning Our Callings in Life*. Grand Rapids: Eerdmans, 2003.

Semuels, Alana. "When Robots Take Bad Jobs." *The Atlantic*, February 17, 2017. https://www.theatlantic.com/business/archive/2017/02/when-robots-take-bad-jobs/517953/.

Sherman, Amy. *Kingdom Calling: Vocational Stewardship for the Common Good*. Downers Grove, IL: InterVarsity, 2011.

Smith, Gordon T. *Called to be Saints: An Invitation to Christian Maturity*. Downers Grove, IL: IVP Academic, 2014.

———. *Courage & Calling: Embracing Your God-Given Potential*. Downers Grove, IL: InterVarsity, 1999.

Smith, James K. A. *Desiring the Kingdom: Worship, Worldview, and Cultural Formation*. Grand Rapids: Baker Academic, 2009.

Stevens, R. Paul. *Aging Matters: Finding Your Calling for the Rest of Your Life*. Grand Rapids: Eerdmans, 2016.

———. *The Other Six Days: Vocation, Work, and Ministry in Biblical Perspective*. Grand Rapids: Eerdmans, 1999.

Sullivan, Kate. "Sarah Sanders: God 'Wanted Donald Trump to Become President.'" CNN, January 31, 2019. https://www.cnn.com/2019/01/30/politics/sarah-sanders-god-trump/index.html.

Taddonio, Patrice. "'You're Just Disposable': New Accounts from Former Amazon Employees Raise Questions about Working Conditions." PBS Frontline, February 14, 2020. https://www.pbs.org/wgbh/frontline/article/youre-just-disposable-new-accounts-from-former-amazon-employees-raise-questions-about-working-conditions/.

Taylor, Charles. *A Secular Age*. Cambridge, MA: Belknap, 2007.

———. *The Sources of the Self: The Making of the Modern Identity*. New York: Cambridge University Press, 1989.

Terkel, Studs. *Working: People Talk about What They Do All Day and How They Feel about What They Do*. New York: New Press, 1997.

Thate, Michael J., Kevin J. Vanhoozer, and Constantine R. Campbell, eds. *"In Christ" in Paul: Explorations in Paul's Theology of Union and Participation*. Grand Rapids: Eerdmans, 2014.

Thomas, Dana Isaiah. *A Higher Calling: Claiming God's Best for Your Life*. Grand Rapids: Zondervan, 2018.

Tickle, Phyllis. *The Great Emergence: How Christianity Is Changing and Why*. Grand Rapids: Baker Books, 2012.

Tripp, Paul David. *Dangerous Calling: Confronting the Unique Challenges of Pastoral Ministry*. Wheaton: Crossway, 2012.

U.S. Bureau of Labor Statistics. "National Longitudinal Surveys: Number of Jobs Held in a Lifetime." August 2019. https://www.bls.gov/nls/questions-and-answers.htm#anch41.

Vanhoozer, Kevin J. "From 'Blessed in Christ' to 'Being in Christ.'" In *"In Christ" in Paul: Explorations in Paul's Theology of Union and Participation*, edited by Michael J. Thate, Kevin J. Vanhoozer, and Constantine R. Campbell, 3–36. Grand Rapids: Eerdmans, 2014.

Volf, Miroslav. *Work in the Spirit: Toward a Theology of Work*. Eugene, OR: Wipf & Stock, 2001.

Waalkes, Scott. "Rethinking Work as Vocation: From Protestant Advice to Gospel Corrective." *Christian Scholar's Review* 44 (2015): 135–53.

Ward, Angie. *I Am a Leader: When Women Discover the Joy of Their Calling*. Colorado Springs: NavPress, 2020.

Weber, Max. *The Protestant Ethic and the Spirit of Capitalism*. New York: Routledge, 1992.

Williams, Reggie L. *Bonhoeffer's Black Jesus: Harlem Renaissance Theology and an Ethic of Resistance*. Waco: Baylor University Press, 2014.

Wilson, Todd. *More: Find Your Personal Calling and Live Life to the Fullest Measure*. Grand Rapids: Zondervan, 2016.

Wingren, Gustaf. *Luther on Vocation*. Translated by Carl C. Rasmussen. Originally published in 1957. Repr., Eugene, OR: Wipf & Stock, 2004.

Winstanley, Gerrard. "A Declaration from the Poor Oppressed People of England." In Placher, *Callings*, 300–303.

Woodhead, Linda. "Theology and the Fragmentation of the Self." *International Journal of Systematic Theology* 1 (1999): 53–72.

Scripture Index

Author Index

Subject Index